I0232689

Costume of Prelates of the Catholic Church

According to Roman Etiquette

By John Abel Felix Prosper Nainfa

I have loved, O Lord, the beauty of Thy house, and the place where Thy glory dwelleth. - Ps. xxv. 8.

PANTIANOS
CLASSICS

Published by Pantianos Classics

ISBN-13: 978-1-78987-547-8

First published in 1926

Contents

Foreword

The encouraging success obtained by the first edition of this Manual prompts its author to offer it again, in a somewhat altered form, to interested, readers who will find in its pages considerable new matter. Pius X.'s Constitution *Sapienti consilio,* reorganizing the administration of the Roman Curia, the promulgation of the new Code of Canon Law, and numerous answers and decrees of the Sacred Congregation of Rites, have made many changes necessary, and I have also received and inserted some valuable suggestions kindly offered by several Prelates.

My sincere thanks go to all who have in any way helped and encouraged me in this undertaking, and particularly to the many Prelates and liturgists who have, verbally or in writing, praised the purpose and contents of the book. Success has crowned this work, in spite of the good-natured predictions of failure which greeted its inception; friendly criticism has not been wanting, it is always most welcome; I have received it with gratitude and availed myself of it when practicable. Occasionally also have I had the surprise to read some portions of this book, given as original productions, over the signatures of genial, if not over-scrupulous, authors; forgetting however the unpleasant feeling, I prefer, for this once, to regard plagiarism, like imitation, as the best kind of flattery.

Now as in the past, I shall gratefully accept suggestions or corrections, and willingly place my little experience of the subjects treated in these pages at the disposal of priests and Prelates for assistance in the solution of practical difficulties which so many regulations of etiquette, precedence and costume may, at times, present or create.

John Abel Nainfa, S. S.

Baltimore, 23 *February* 1925.

Preface to the First Edition

The contents of this little book will be new, doubtless, to most readers. Indeed, the first reason that prompted its composition was the fact that there is not in the English language any other work on this subject.

Really, if we except the important writings of Mgr. Barbier de Montault, we find scarcely anything treating *ex professo* of this matter. The works of this learned Prelate deserve the reputation they enjoy; for they are a mine of erudition. The information they furnish is, as a rule, remarkable for its accuracy. It seems, however, that a serious lack of order, numerous and useless digressions, and the aggressive tone in which these works have been written, have proved a serious hindrance to their popularity.

To this first reason, rather negative, for its publication, I might add a second, that of positive utility. With the exception of Italy, there is no other country in which the proportion of Prelates is larger than in the United States. Now these Prelates would naturally desire to have their official costume conform as far as possible to the rules and prescriptions of the Church with regard to its color, shape, trimmings, etc. They will find this manual at least useful as a book of reference in matter of the costume which they are privileged to wear.

Such a manual seems almost a necessity when we remember that tailors, in making ecclesiastical costumes, very often follow their own tastes, fancies, or designs instead of the very clear and precise rules of ecclesiastical etiquette. With this manual in hand, they would have no longer an excuse for the mistakes they make.

Even our good Sisters and pious ladies, who so kindly and generously shower Christmas presents on the Clergy, in the shape of birettas, "rabbis", surplices, cottas, and other articles of clerical dress, need to be informed that the material, color, shape, trimmings, etc., of these objects are regulated not by the rich taste, generous liberality or devotion of the giver, but by ordinances of the Church.

May I not hope, then, that this little book, in spite of its shortcomings and imperfections, will prove useful to those interested, and be a guide where needed in the making up of ecclesiastical costumes?

With regard to the various costumes worn by Prelates, the will of the Church has been that modifications, however excellent and, in some way, justifiable, should not be left to private fancy; for she clearly foresaw that, after a short lapse of years, such toleration would practically do away with a unity at once beautiful and instructive.

Therefore has she laid down for all these costumes precise regulations that should not be lightly put aside. Two Roman Congregations, the Congregation of Rites and the Congregation of the Ceremonial, are especially commissioned to watch over the exact observance of these rules and to secure their preservation.

It is to the decrees of these two Congregations that I have chiefly had recourse in compiling this manual. The decrees of the Congregation of Rites are quoted from the Collections of Gardellini and Muhlbauer. As to the Decrees of the Congregation of the Ceremonial, as there exists no official Collection, I have had to rely on the authors who quote them. To the decrees, I have joined the prescriptions of the Ceremonials, and especially of the official books of the Church, the Missal, the Ceremonial of Bishops, and the Roman Pontifical, which contain a wealth of interesting and instructive Rubrics.

Finally, for the interpretation of decrees and rubrics, and for the modern adaptation of all these rules, I have consulted authors generally considered the best, who have devoted their lives to original research in this matter, such as Mgr. Martinucci – "Rex Caeremoniariorum" - Mgr. Barbier de Montault, the Rev. Fr. Haegy, C. S. Sp., in his new edition of "Les Cérémonies Pontificales" of the learned Father Levavasseur, etc.

As to matter that is not to be found in books, I have invariably followed Roman Tradition, the only one of authority on this point as on all others.

It goes without saying that I have not failed to mention lawful customs where these exist.

Before closing these few remarks, it is my duty to acknowledge my debt of gratitude to all who have in any way been a help to me in rendering this small volume less unworthy of its readers. They have my sincere thanks.

I add that I shall gratefully accept any suggestions that might aid me to improve this first essay, and declare that all the contents of this book, both in general and particular, are respectfully and cheer fully submitted to the judgment of ecclesiastical authority.

J. A. Nainfa, S. S.

Baltimore, February 18, 1909.

Part I - General Principles

Chapter One - Prelature

1. The word "Prelate" (from *praeferre,* to put before) is a general name for an ecclesiastical dignitary who has jurisdiction *in foro externo,* whether he be a member of the secular or of the regular clergy; his jurisdiction not being delegated, but inherent in the office he holds. [1]

Prelature (or *Prelacy*) is the status of a Prelate. This term applies to the honor given to a dignitary on account of the jurisdiction with which he is invested.

This is the canonical sense of the words *Prelate* and *Prelature.* In a wider sense, these designations are extended to other dignitaries of various kinds who have no special jurisdiction, but are personally granted the title and honors of Prelates, namely the members of the Pope's Court and Household. In this sense, the words *Prelate* and *Prelature* mean nothing else than a superiority of rank. [2]

In this manual, we use the word *Prelate* particularly in a *liturgical sense.* By *Prelate,* we understand a dignitary of the Catholic Church, who is entitled to wear a special costume, and whose rank deserves special honors, both in every-day life and in liturgical functions.

2. The teaching of the Council of Trent is that the Hierarchy [3] of the Church is, by divine institution, composed of three elements, Bishops, Priests and Ministers. [4]

This simple division having been found insufficient in proportion as Christianity spread, the Church was led to create intermediary offices which, without interfering with the primitive division, constituted supplementary degrees, with the view of making the external administration of the Church easier and more effective. For instance, we see the institution of Metropolitans, [5] of Patriarchs, [6] the gradual growth in the importance of the Sacred College, [7] etc. Thus, alongside of the Hierarchy of Order, divinely instituted, grew up the Hierarchy, of administration, or of *Jurisdiction,* as it is called. Both together, harmoniously combined, form that admirable organization, the Catholic Hierarchy. [8]

Moreover, Popes, desirous of showing their satisfaction or good will towards certain members of the Clergy, invested them with the title and honors of a higher rank, without however investing them with the functions pertaining to that rank, as, for instance, the Latin incumbents of the Eastern Patriarchates, the titular Archbishops and Bishops, the honorary Prelates of the Papal Court, etc.

3. When a man is raised to an ecclesiastical dignity, the only rule of conduct proper for Catholics to follow is to recognize the new dignitary as such, and to give him the honors due to his rank.

But this rank must be indicated in some manner, so that the faithful may recognize it and pay it due honor. For this purpose, the Church has assigned a special costume to various Prelates. Now, the obligation of a Prelate is correlative. Since it is the duty of the faithful to pay due respect to his dignity, the Prelate is reciprocally bound to make his dignity known by wearing the proper costume. x Owing to personal sentiments of humility, one may sometimes be opposed to this solemn display; but the example given by great saints like the noble Cardinal St. Charles Borromeo, and the holy Bishop, St. Francis de Sales, who were scrupulously faithful in observing the least prescriptions of the Ceremonials, proves that such humility has no legitimate foundation.

4. If an objection is raised on the score of the anti-democratic appearance of the Church dignities, our only answer is that dignities are not in opposition to the democratic spirit of a people if they are within the reach of all. Such is the case for the dignities of the Church, in which "the son of a peasant may reach the pontifical throne as well as a prince who has the prestige of wealth and noble blood." [10]

[1] Benedict XIV., de *syn. diaec.*, Book II., ch. XI. Bouix, de *Episc.* Tom. I., pp. 535, seq. Taunton, *The Law of the Church*, art. Prelate, p. 499.

[2] Frequently, authors use the words *Prelature* and *Prelacy* to designate all Prelates taken as a body.

[3] The word Hierarchy is taken here in its proper canonical meaning of *a body of clergy of different ranks or orders, enjoying* ecclesiastical powers *according to their several degrees.* The commonly received meaning of the word *Hierarchy*, namely that of "the body of the Bishops of a country," is incorrect.

[4] *"If anyone say that, in the Catholic Church, there is not a hierarchy, instituted by divine authority, which consists of Bishops, Priests, and Ministers, let him be anathema."* (Council of Trent, Session XXIII., can. 2.)

[5] Phillips, *Du droit ecclésiastique*, Tom. II., p. 63.

[6] Phillips, op. cit., Tom. II., pp. 25, seq. Council of Nicaea, *can.* VI.

[7] Ferraris, *Bibliotheca*, art. *Cardinales.*

[8] Taunton, *The Law of the Church*, Art. Hierarchy, pp. 358, 359. - Ferraris, *Bibliotheca canonica*, art. *Hierarchia ecclesiastica.*

[9] When a privilege is granted to a class of dignitaries, each one of them is bound to make use of the privilege; otherwise, he wrongs the body of which he is a member. Moreover, he has no right to refuse a privilege the concession of which has been made rather to the body than to himself individually.

[10] P. A. Baart, *The Roman Court*, p. 333.

II. Prelates

The different classes of Prelates who are the subjects of this preliminary chapter are: The Pope, who is the supreme Prelate; the Cardinals, Patriarchs, Archbishops and Bishops, Regular Prelates and Prelates of the Roman Court.

The Pope

Every Catholic knows who the Pope is and the high rank he holds in the Church. He is the Bishop of Bishops," [1] the "Prelate of Prelates." He possesses supreme and infallible authority to teach and govern the Church. He is above laws and canons, [2] and, though he has been despoiled of his temporal power, he is still recognized as a Sovereign by nearly all civilized nations.

In the present study, we have but to remark that the Pope, being the Supreme Prelate, wears a special prelatical costume, and that certain materials and colors are reserved for him, as we shall note later.

The Cardinals

The Cardinals are those Prelates who form the Senate of the Church. Their name, from the Latin word *cardo* (a hinge), seems to indicate that the government of the Church rests on them as a door on its hinges. [3]

They are divided into three classes: Cardinal-Bishops, Cardinal-Priests and Cardinal-Deacons; [4] but this distinction does not proceed from their ordination; an Archbishop as, for instance, the Archbishop of Paris, usually is a Cardinal-Priest; and a Cardinal-Deacon must now be a priest in orders: the distinction originates in their *titles;* for the cardinalitial dignity does not belong to the Hierarchy of Order, but to that of Jurisdiction. [5]

The *title* of a Cardinal is taken from the diocese or the church to which he is appointed as Cardinal; but ordinarily the word "*title*" is used only to mean the churches assigned to Cardinal-Priests. The episcopal sees of Cardinal-Bishops are usually called "*suburban dioceses.*" [6]

These dioceses, located in the *suburbs* of Rome (hence their name) form the Roman metropolitan province. They are:

OSTIA and VELETRI, the Bishop of which is the Dean of the Sacred College;

PORTO and SANTA RUFINA, a see formerly reserved for the Sub-Dean of the Sacred College;

SABINA, which is not a city, but a territory;

PALESTRINA, the Bishop of which is entitled *Praenestinus Episcopus;*

PRASCATI, formerly Tusculum, a name which has been preserved in the title of the Bishop, who is styled *Tusculanus Episcopus;*

ALBANO, *Albanensis Episcopus.*

Each Cardinal -Priest has for title one of the churches of the city of Rome, which was formerly a parish church. The title of a Cardinal-Deacon is also a church, but generally one which has been used as the chapel of a hospital or asylum, the deacons functions consisting in providing for the necessities of the poor. This "title" is, even at the present day, called *Diaconia* (Deaconry). [7]

As a body, the Cardinals are known as the *Sacred College*. The College is headed by the Dean, who is the first of the Cardinal-Bishops in order of seniority, and always Bishop of Ostia and Veletri.

The Cardinals functions generally consist in acting as advisers [8] and auxiliaries to the Sovereign Pontiff in the administration of the Church. They also govern the Church during the vacancy of the Holy See and elect the new Pope. [9]

Their official title is *"Eminentissimus et Reverendissimus Dominus,"* [10] and their dignity gives them a right of precedence immediately after the Pope and over all those who are not Cardinals. [11]

They enjoy a great many special privileges which are noted in the Code of Canon Law, Can. 239.

Patriarchs and Primates

Although, by divine institution and ordination, Bishops are all equal, yet Ecclesiastical Law has introduced certain modifications in episcopal authority, by virtue of which, some Bishops are superior to others, exercising over them a real authority, a participation, as it were, of the supreme Prelacy of the Sovereign Pontiff. Such are *Patriarchs, Primates, Archbishops* or *Metropolitans.* [12]

Literally, the word *Patriarch* means a "Chief of Fathers. The appellation is very ancient. The title of the early Bishops being that of "Father, their leaders were quite naturally called "Patriarchs.

This title of Patriarch was first given to the Bishops of Rome, Alexandria and Antioch, three episcopal sees the foundation of which is ascribed to St. Peter. [13]

To these three patriarchal sees were soon added the bishopric of Jerusalem, on account of the life, death, and resurrection of our Lord, and the bishopric of Constantinople, on account of the new importance given to the city as the residence of the Roman Emperor. [14]

But since the cities, in which the Eastern patriarchal sees were established, have fallen under the domination of infidels or schismatics, the Popes, in order to keep alive the memory of these illustrious sees, have continued to appoint Latin Patriarchs, who enjoy not only the titles of these sees, but the prerogatives and privileges of the patriarchal rank as well. However, they have no jurisdiction over the territory of their patriarchates. These great Prelates are called "Titular Patriarchs." [15] Pius IX. made an exception to the usual practice, when he allowed the Latin Patriarch of Jerusalem a residence in his patriarchal city, and invested him with metropolitan jurisdiction over Jerusalem and its vicinity. [16]

Besides these Latin patriarchs, there are, in the East, Catholic patriarchs of the different rites, all of them having over their subjects the same traditional authority as the ancient patriarchs of the Eastern Church. Such are: the Patriarch of Antioch for the *Melchites,* residence at Damascus; the Patriarch of Alexandria for the *Copts,* residence at Cairo (Egypt); the Patriarch of Antioch for the *Maronites,* residence at Bikorchi (Lebanon); the Patriarch of Antioch for the *Syrians,* residence also at Bikorchi; the Patriarch of Babylon f or the *Chaldeans,* residence at Mossul (Mesopotamia), and the Patriarch of Cilicia for the *Armenians,* residence at Constantinople. [17]

Several Bishops in the Western Church have also been granted the title and honors of Patriarchs. These are the Patriarch of Venice (Italy); the Patriarch of Lisbon (Portugal); the Patriarch of the West Indies, who is the Chaplain General of the Spanish Army (usually the Archbishop of Toledo, Spain); and the Patriarch of the East Indies, who is the Archbishop of Goa in India. [18] These are known as Minor Patriarchs.

Primates were Bishops having authority or jurisdiction over the Archbishops of a country or of a considerable portion of a country. Nowadays, the jurisdiction of Primates has practically ceased, though some Bishops have kept the title, a merely honorary one. Such, for instance, are the Archbishop of Armagh, Primate of All Ireland; the Archbishop of Dublin, "Primate of Ireland; the Archbishop of Lyons, "Primate of Gaul; the Archbishop of Gran, "Primate of Hungary," etc. [19]

In the Eastern Church, the corresponding title was that of *Exarch.* [20]

Primates have no special privilege with regard to the prelatical costume; but Patriarchs possess a certain number of distinctions which mark externally their high dignity: All Patriarchs are Assistants at the Pontifical throne; they rank immediately after the Cardinals, and have the privilege of wearing, even in Rome, the *mozzetta* over the *mantelletta;* their winter cloaks are adorned with a border of gold; etc. In Rome, they have the prerogative of consecrating Bishops, if there is no Cardinal at hand to perform the ceremony. [21]

Archbishops and Bishops

This is not the proper place to treat of the origin of the archiepiscopal dignity. Suffice it to say that an Archbishop is a Prelate invested with the episcopal character, and holding a rank immediately superior to that of simple Bishops.

An Archbishop is also called a Metropolitan," from the ancient custom of calling the Bishop of the capital (*metropolis*) of a Roman province *metropolitanus.* [22] The title of Metropolitan is not however given to titular Archbishops, since they have no ordinary jurisdiction over an ecclesiastical province.

The proper insignia of a Metropolitan Archbishop are the *pallium* [23] and the *cross.* [24]

The *pallium* (or pall) consists of a circular band of white lamb's wool, from which hang two pendants of the same material, one of which is meant to fall down the middle of the back, and the other over the center of the breast. Six little black crosses are embroidered on the band and its lappets. The pallium is worn over the chasuble at pontifical Mass, on certain days determined by the Ceremonial of Bishops. (*Caer. Ep.* I., XVI, 3, 4).

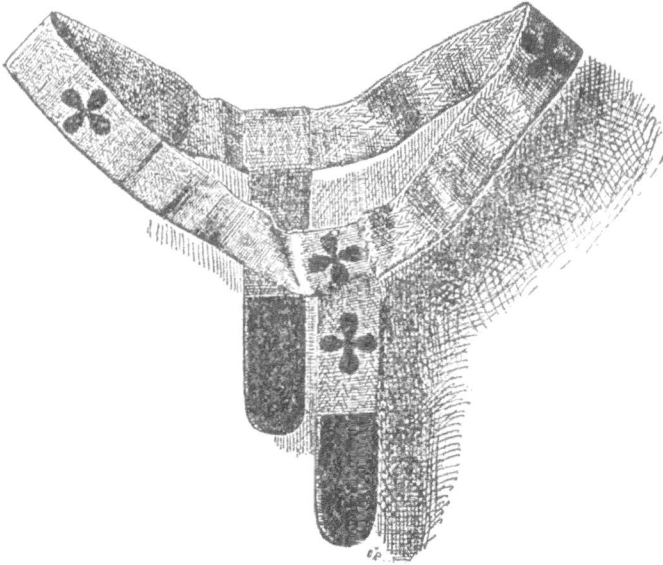

Pallium

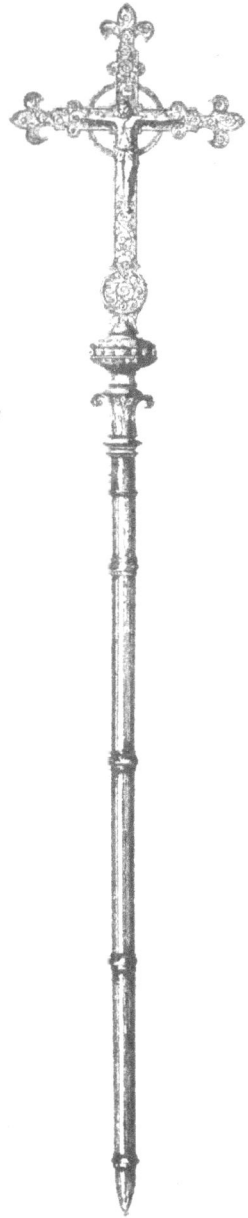

The "metropolitan cross," commonly, though improperly, called "archiepiscopal cross," is much like the processional cross, [25] and is held or carried by a Subdeacon, or a member of the Prelate's house hold, in such a way that the crucifix is always turned towards the Prelate. [26]

The pallium and the cross, being tokens of jurisdiction, should not be used outside of the Province over which the Archbishop has authority. [27] For this reason, titular Archbishops do not make use of either the cross or the pallium, since they have no territorial jurisdiction.

Metropolitan Cross

A Bishop (a word derived from the Greek ἐπίσχοπος "*overseer*") is an ecclesiastical dignitary who has received, through his consecration, the full priestly character, and has the special charge of governing a determined portion of the Christian flock under the supervision of the Sovereign Pontiff. [28]

An Archbishop or a Bishop is called *residential* when he occupies a see canonically erected, with residence in and ordinary jurisdiction over the limited territory annexed to the city from which the see takes its name.

He is styled *titular* when he has no ordinary jurisdiction over the diocese of which he bears the title, his episcopal or archiepiscopal see being under the domination of infidels or schismatics. [29] Formerly, Titular Bishops or Archbishops were also styled "Bishops (or Archbishops) *in partibus infidelium*" (in the countries of infidels); but, yielding to the protests of the Greek government, under whose domination many of these titular sees are located, Pope Leo XIII, abolished the title of Bishop *in partibus infidelium*," and decreed that henceforth only the title of Titular Bishop (or Archbishop) of N. in N." (the name of the episcopal city, with that of the ancient Roman province to which the city belonged) should be used: Thus Right Reverend *N. N. N., Titular Bishop of Rosea in Cilicia.*" [30]

Archbishops and Bishops, when promoted to the rank of "Assistants at the Pontifical Throne, become members of the Papal household. They obtain the privilege of a special place at the Papal *"chapels,"* [31] where they act as book-bearer and candle-bearer, and have the right of celebrating pontifical Mass in presence of the Pope. Together with the brief of appointment, they receive from the Secretariate of State a diploma written on parchment, giving the full list of their rights and privileges many of which have fallen into disuse, especially those regarding the conferring of benefices. [32]

As members of the Papal Court, the Assistants at the Pontifical Throne are entitled to wear its insignia, namely, silk clothes in summer. But that privilege is conceded only for the time which they actually spend in Rome; their title of "Assistants" giving them no right of precedence or distinction among the other Bishops, except at the Roman Court. [33]

The title is very seldom granted motu propn o, because the Roman Court wishes the precept retained, Ask and you shall receive. But, if a Bishop makes application, the title is bestowed upon him without the slightest difficulty. [34]

Together with the title of "Assistant at the Pontifical Throne," the Bishop generally receives that of *Roman Count,* that is *"Count of the Apostolic Palace and of the Lateran Court."* [35]

Regular Prelates

In Canon Law, the title of *"Regular Prelate"* is given to a religious superior having over his subjects a quasi-episcopal jurisdiction. [36]

Here, we take the title as that of a Prelate (in the broad, liturgical sense of this word) belonging to a Religious Order; and this practically includes only Cardinals, Bishops and Abbots.

The Cardinals and Bishops who are taken from a Religious Order still remain substantially bound by their religious vows, as far as these are not in opposition to their duties and dignity as Prelates. [37]

According to the old Common Law, they should continue to wear the habit of their Order, and they remain now free to do so if they prefer. However, the custom of using the same form as that of the secular Prelates costume is tolerated. The color of the prelatical dress is the same as that of the religious habit, unless otherwise determined by the traditions of the Order (as, for instance, the Franciscans), or by special concessions and regulations of the Holy See. [38]

The different costumes of Prelates taken from Religious Orders have been regulated as follows:

Clerics Regular, i.e. those who have adopted the new type of religious life inaugurated in the sixteenth century, as Theatines, Barnabites, Jesuits, Oratorians, Passionists, Redemptorists, Paulists, etc., when appointed Cardinals or Bishops, adopt the costume of secular Prelates, [39] because they are looked upon as such; with this restriction, however, that they have no right to make use of silk, except for the trimmings and accessories of their costume. [40]

Cardinals and Bishops belonging to the Orders of St. Basil, of Vallombrosa, and of the Regular Canons and Hermits of St. Augustine (*Augustinians*) wear an entirely black costume. [41]

The prelatical dress of the Benedictines is black with red lining and trimmings. The cloak (*ferraiolone*), however, should be entirely black. [42]

The monks of St. Sylvester, when promoted to Prelacy, dress in a dark blue costume.

The Carthusians, the Camaldules, the Premonstratensians, the members of the Orders of Our Lady of Mercy and of the Holy Trinity, and the Olivetans, wear a prelatical costume entirely white.

The Cistercians and the Reformed Cistercians (Trappists) wear cassock, simar, cincture, collaro and stockings made of white material; but the *mozzetta, mantelletta* and cloak (*ferraiolone*) are black. The *cappa magna* is also black, with a cape of ermine in winter and of white silk in summer. The color of the trimmings conforms to that of the different portions of the costume.

The Prelates belonging to the Order of St. Dominic dress in the same colors as the Cistercians, but the trimmings, lining and buttons are all white, even for the black portions of the costume.

Franciscans, when promoted to Prelacy, lay aside the brown, or black material of their habit, and vest in a dress of ash-colored gray (a color which contemporary paintings ascribe to the habit worn by St. Francis). The *cappa magna* of these Prelates is of the same color, and is furred, in winter, with vicunia's skin.

Alone in the Franciscan family, the Capuchins do not change the color of their dress when becoming Prelates. The winter cape of the *cappa magna* is made of otter's fur.

Carmelite Prelates retain in their costume the two colors, brown and white, of the religious habit of the Order. The cassock, simar and cincture are brown; the *mozzetta, mantelletta, ferraiolo* or *ferraiolone* and *cappa magna*,

15

white. The Cardinals belonging to the Order have the privilege of wearing this costume lined and trimmed in purple, with purple stockings and a purple cincture.

All Cardinals, both secular and regular, wear the proper insignia of the Cardinalate - hat, biretta, and skull cap of scarlet silk without regard to the color of their habit. [43]

Likewise, Archbishops and Bishops, whatever their origin, are all entitled to wear the hat with green cordons and tassels, [44] the purple biretta [45] and skull-cap, [46] these being the proper insignia of the episcopal office.

Abbots

There are two classes of Abbots, the Abbots *nullius* and the Abbots *regiminis* or "Simple Abbots."

The Abbots nullius *diaeceseos* (i.e., belonging to no diocese), usually called Abbots nullius, are those who have full jurisdiction over a certain territory and its inhabitants, with absolute exemption from the authority of any Bishop. [47]

Simple Abbots are those who have jurisdiction in their monastery and its annexed territory, though this territory is within the limits of a diocese, the Bishop of which has a right of supervision, precedence and interference in the monastery itself. [48]

Both classes of Abbots, though not invested with the episcopal character, possess the privilege of using the "pontificals," [49] with this difference, that the Abbots *nullius* are allowed their use at all times and without restrictions, while the privilege of simple Abbots is limited by law and by the presence of the diocesan Bishop. In an Abbey *nullius,* a Bishop is always considered "outside of his diocese," even if the territory of the Abbey is enclosed in his own diocesan territory; while, on the contrary, in a simple Abbey, the Bishop, in whose diocese the Abbey is located, is in his diocese. [50]

Abbots *regiminis,* as well as Abbots nullius, add to their monastic habit the pectoral cross and the ring. [51]

They have also the privilege of vesting in the *mozzetta* when acting within the limits of their territory, and the *mantelletta* when they are outside. The *mozzetta* and *mantelletta* are of the same color as the religious habit. [52] Regularly speaking, they should not make use of the rochet; but ordinarily this is conceded by special favor of the Holy See. [53]

An Abbot *nullius* in his territory may wear the *cappa magna* [54] of the same shape and color as the Bishops belonging to the Order; but this vestment, if not personally conceded, can not lawfully be worn by simple Abbots.

All Abbots, without regard to the color of their monastic habit, are free to wear a black hat with cords and tassels of the same color, and also a black biretta and a black skull-cap. As will be seen in the chapter on Heraldry, they place a hat, with three rows of tassels on each side, over the shield of their arms; this hat is always black, irrespective of the color of the monastic habit; but a recently introduced custom allows Abbots *nullius* to use the same green heraldic hat as Bishops, on account of their quasi-episcopal jurisdiction.

The above principles are far from exhaustive; but the reader must remember that each monastic order enjoys a considerable number of special privileges coming from immemorial traditions or apostolic indults, which cannot find place in this volume.

Prelates of the Roman Court

The Pope, Cardinals, Patriarchs, Primates, Arch bishops, Bishops and Abbots are properly and canonically called "*Prelates*." But, besides these, there is, in the Roman Church, a class of officials invested by the Pope with the title and dignity of Prelates, who are commonly entitled "Roman Prelates," or "Prelates of the Roman Court,' *Romanae Curiae Antistites.*

Formerly, these Prelates were simply the officers of the Papal Court, composing the household of the Sovereign Pontiff, or filling different offices in the "Congregations. Little by little, especially during the last century, the number of these Prelates was largely increased by the conferring upon priests the title and honors attached to these offices, without, however, granting these new dignitaries any part in the general administration of the Church.

These honorary dignities, bestowed upon a priest, give him the title and honors attached to them, with a determined precedence over certain other classes of ecclesiastics; but do not affect his jurisdiction.

The papal household is composed of two classes of Prelates: the Prelates *di mantelletta* and the Prelates *di mantellone* so called from the kind of official garment they wear. The Prelates *di mantelletta* are really "Prelates," their title is personal and their appointment is for life. Their Prelature is something permanent, and they can be dismissed only for unworthiness or crime, after a regular trial, or *motu proprio,* by a positive act of the Sovereign Pontiff.

The Prelates *di mantellone* enjoy the title and honors of Prelates, though they are not Prelates in reality. Their "Prelature" is simply an office or an honor attached to an office, and it does not affect their personality; nor is it permanent, though they are not dismissed except for serious cause; but they lose their title and their office on the Pope's death, because they are regarded as his personal officers, and his successor is not bound to keep the same attendants.

When the new Pope is elected, they may apply for a renewal of their Prelacy, and the favor is generally granted without any difficulty. But, during the vacancy of the Holy See, and until they are reinstated by the newly-elected Pope, they must faithfully abstain from wearing the costume proper to the office or dignity which they have lost.

The Patriarchs, Archbishops and Bishops Assistants at the Pontifical Throne, and the Prelates *di mantelletta,* essentially constitute the household of the Sovereign Pontiff, hence their general title of "Domestic Prelates."

17

If the Prelates *di mantelletta* belong to a "College," [55] they bear the title especially attributed to the members of that College; if they do not belong to a College, they are simply given the general title of *Domestic Prelates*.

The different Colleges of Domestic Prelates are:

The Patriarchs,

The Archbishops and Bishops Assistants at the Pontifical Throne,

The Protonotaries [56] Apostolic,

The *Votantes* of the Signature, [57]

The Referees of the Signature,

The Auditors of the Rota,

The Clerks of the Rev. Chamber Apostolic.

After these *Prelates,* come those who do not belong to a College, styled in general *"Domestic Prelates."*

There are four classes of Protonotaries Apostolic:-

1. The Protonotaries Apostolic *de numero participantium,* i.e., of the number of the participating, generally reckoned as Protonotaries Apostolic *di numero,"* who form a "College" of seven Prelates, acting as official Notaries to the Sovereign Pontiff.

2. The Protonotaries Apostolic Supernumerary, who obtain their title from being appointed Canons of certain Roman Basilicas.

3. The Protonotaries Apostolic *ad instar participantium* (or, more usually, *"ad instar"*), who may obtain their title either by their appointment as Canons of certain Cathedrals, the Chapter of which have been granted such privilege, or - and this is the general rule - from being raised to that dignity by the Sovereign Pontiff. The Prelates, known as "Protonotaries Apostolic" in this country, belong to this third class of Protonotaries.

4. The Titular (or Honorary) Protonotaries Apostolic," also called "Black Protonotaries, are not members of the Pontifical Household; they enjoy the privileges of the prelatical rank only outside of the City of Rome, and, as will be said later, their prelatial dress is entirely black, without any addition of red or purple.

Such Protonotaries are nowadays very seldom, if ever, directly appointed by the Pope. But, since 1905, the title and honors of Titular Protonotaries Apostolic belong, *pleno iure,* to the Vicars General of Bishops, and to the Vicars Capitular or Administrators of vacant dioceses, if these dignitaries are not Prelates otherwise.

The important privileges peculiar to the different classes of Protonotaries Apostolic have been recently modified, and are all expressed in the Constitution *Inter multiplices,* issued *motu proprio* by Pope Pius X., on February 21, 1905. Therefore, all manuals treating of the subject should be corrected according to the regulations of that document. [58]

The other Prelatial Colleges consist of Prelates who hold offices with practical functions in Roman Congregations and Tribunals, and are bound to reside in Rome.

After these, come those Prelates *di mantelletta,* who have been much increased numerically in these last years, who belong to no College, and, therefore, are simply called "Domestic Prelates."

As has been said, the Prelates *di mantellone* are the attendants on the person of the Holy Father. They belong to two different classes, *Chamberlains* and *Chaplains.*

Those who have to fulfill real functions in the Vatican Palace are styled participating or "*di numero,*" the others are *supernumerary* or *honorary.*

Their order of precedence is as follows:

Private Chamberlains participating.
Private Chamberlains supernumerary.
Private Chamberlains of honor *in abito paonazzo.* [59]
Private Chamberlains *extra Urbem* (outside the city).
Private Chaplains participating.
Private Chaplains of honor.
Private Chaplains *extra Urbem* (outside the city).
The Six Common Chaplains participating.
Common Chaplains supernumerary.

All these Prelates wear the same costume, and are given the same marks of honor. However, those entitled *extra Urbem,* that is, "outside the City of Rome," are never allowed to make use of their prelatical privileges in Rome. They could do so only in the presence of the Pope, should he happen temporarily to reside outside of Rome, as was quite often done before the invasion of the Pontifical States.

All that regards the costumes of these Prelates will be found hereafter in the Chapter which treats of the *Mantellone.*

The classes of Prelates are so numerous that, though only a few lines have been devoted to each, this chapter has taken on unusual length. This, however, was necessary, as in the succeeding chapters, constant allusions and references will be made to these various classes of Prelates, allusions and references which would not be easily understood without the general notions just indicated.

[1] Tertullian, de *pudicitia,* I., 6.
[2] Council of the Vatican, Const. *Pastor aeternus,* c. 2, 3, 4.
[3] Soglia, *Institutiones iuris publici,* Part. II., 41, and others.
[4] Soglia, *ibid.* Bouix, de *curia romana,* p. 1, etc. Codex Juris Canonici, 231.
[5] Ferraris, *Bibliotheca canonica, ad art. Cardinales,* II. Codex Juris Canonici, 232.
[6] Soglia, op. et loc. cit. BouiX, loc. cit.

[7] Ferraris, *Bibliotheca,* art. *Cardinales,* I. - Sixtus V., Constit. *Postquam* (Dec. 3, 1586).
[8] Council of Trent, Session xxv., Chapt. I., de *reformatione.*
[9] Codex Juris Canonici, 241.
[10] Decree of Pope Urban VIII. (June 10, 1630).
[11] Eugène IV., Constit. *Non mediocri.*
[12] Bouix, de *curia romana.* - Soglia, *Instit. iur. publ.,* part. II., etc. - Codex, Liber II. Pars I., cap. III.

[13] Phillips, *Da droit ecclésiastique,* Tome II., p. 25.
[14] Phillips, *loc. cit.*
[15] Bennettis, *Privil. S. Petri,* p. 134. Phillips, *op. cit.,* Tome II., p. 45.
[16] Constit. *Nulla celebrior,* July 22, 1847 (Pius IX.).
[17] Mgr. Battandier, *Annuaire Pontifical,* yearly.
[18] Phillips, *loc. cit.,* p. 47. Battandier, *op. cit.*
[19] Bouix, de *Episc.,* Part. IV., sect. 1, chap. 2.
[20] Ferraris, *Bibliotheca canonica,* art. *Exarchi et Primates.*
[21] Grimaldi, *Les Congrégations romaines,* ch. IX., p. 131. - Mgr. Martinucci, *Man. Caer.,* V., Metropolitan ch. 11. Cross.
[22] Council of Nicaea, can. IV. Bouix, de Episc., Tom. I., pp. 460 *et seq.*
[23] Pontificale Romanum, de *pallio.* Caer. Episc., I., XVI. - Mann, *Lives of the Popes,* Tom. I., Appendix.
[24] Clem. 2. de *privilegiis.* - Thomassin, de *vet. et nova Eccl. discipl.* (*in loco*).
[25] This cross should not be double-armed.
[26] Caer. Episc. I., II. 4. I., IV. 1. II., VIII. 27. II., XXII. 3.I., XV. 2. Mgr. Martinucci, Man. Ger., V., ch. Ill, n. 60, etc.
[27] Codex Juris Canonici., 275-279.
[28] Codex Juris Canonici., 329.
[29] Benedict XIV., de *syn. diaec.,* Book II., eh. VII. Leo XIII., Constit. *In Suprema* (June 4, 1882).
[30] Decree of the *Propaganda* (Febr. 27, 1882.) Leo XIII.'s *Const. cit.*
[31] A "*chapel*" is a religious service at which the Pope officiates or assists.
[32] Grimaldi, *op. cit.,* ch. V., pp. 61, 62. Fisquet, *Cérémonies de Rome* (*passim*). Baron Geramb, *Visit to Rome,* p. 156. T. Pope, *Holy Week in the Vatican,* p. 352.
[33] Mgr. Barbier de Montault, *Le costume et les usages ecclésiastiques,* Tom. I., p. 54.
[34] Grimaldi, *op. cit., ch. V.,* p. 62.
[35] Mgr. Barrier de Montault, *Traité pratique...* Tom. I., p. 473. - Grimaldi, *loc. cit., op. cit.,* ch. xxvii., p. 484. Mgr. A. Battandier, *Annuaire pontifical* (1899, p. 365).
[36] *Cf.* Suarez, de *Relig., tract.* VIII., lib. II., *cap.* II., *num.* 7. Ferraris, *Bibliotheca,* art. *Praelatus regularis* and *Regulares.*
[37] Suarez de *Relig., tract.* VIII.. lib. III., *ch.* XVI. S. C., C, Decemb. 7, 1639.
[38] Ferraris, *Bibliotheca,* art. *Episcopus.* VIII. - *Caer. Episc.* I., I., 4. - According to an immemorial custom, the Legates of the Holy See who belong to religious orders may wear the costume of secular Cardinals. (Mgr. Battandier, *Ann. Pont.,* 1914, p. 121).
[39] *Caer. Episc.* I., III., 4. Martinucci, *Man. Caer.,* V., ch. 11.
[40] Barbier de Montault, *Traité pratique...* Tom. II., p. 524. Martinucci, *loc. cit.,* VI. *Appendix.* - Grimaldi, *op. cit.,* ch. VIII., p. 114.
[41] Barbier de Montault, *op. cit.,* Tom. II., p. 523. - Martinucci, *loc. cit.*
[42] Grimaldi, *op. cit.* ch. VIII., p. 114; ch. XXIX., p. 514.
[43] Gregory XIV., Const. *Sanctissimus.* - Battandier, *Annuaire Pontifical* (1903). p.359.
[44] Car. *Episc.* I., i., 4. Martinucci, *Man. Caer.* V., ch. II., n. 19.
[45] Leo XIII., Const. *Praeclaro divinae gratiae.*
[46] Pius IX., Const. *Ecclesiarum omnium.*
[47] Benedict XIV., de *syn. diaec.,* Book II., ch. XI. Ferraris, *Bibliotheca,* art. *Abbas.* Codex Juris Canonici, Canons 198, 215, 319, 320, 323, 325, etc.
[48] Sebastianelli, de *personis,* p. 350, n. 297. Ferraris, *loc. cit.,* Codex Juris Canonici. Canons 223, 358, 625, 964.
[49] Pius VII., Constit. *Decet Romanum Pontificem,* July 23, 1823.
[50] S.R.C., February 7. 1604.

[51] Pius VII., *Const. cit.* Extensive decree of the S. R. C., Sept. 17. 1659.

[52] Taunton, *The Law of the Church*, Art. "Abbat.," p. 3, n. 10.

[53] S. R. C., Decree of Septemb. 17. 1659, n. 9. Battandier, *Annuaire* (1909),p.421.

[54] Barbier de Montault, *Le costume et les usages ecclésiastiques*, Tom. I., p. 375. Codex Juris Canonici, Canon 325.

[55] The word "College" means a group or assembly of Prelates invested with the same title, enjoying the same honors and privileges, and performing the same functions at the Roman Court.

[56] Throughout this treatise the word Protonotary is spelled without the "h," which is usually inserted. Protonotary is derived from *protos,* first, not from *prothos.* The Latin, Italian, French, Spanish languages retain *proto* in protonotary, just as in protomartyr and similar compound words. Can any good reason be given for writing *prothonotary,* except that some one else has done it? P. A. Baart, *The Roman Court,* Preface.

[57] *Chirographum* of Benedict XV., June 28., 1915.

[58] This important document is given in full in Appendix.

[59] "In purple habit."

Chapter Two - Materials

1. The various materials used for the ecclesiastical costume are, velvet, watered silk, plain silk, broadcloth and other woolen materials, as serge, merino ("*drap d'été*"), etc.

2. *Velvet* is exclusively reserved for the Pope. No ecclesiastic, whatever may be his dignity, is allowed to have any part of his costume made of this material. [1] It is hardly necessary to remark that this principle is opposed to the practice of wearing a velvet biretta, and of ornamenting the cassock with a velvet collar or velvet cuffs.

Some old ceremonials, or other books dealing with ecclesiastical etiquette, generally of French or German origin, assert that velvet cuffs on the purple cassock of Bishops are a privilege of the Assistants at the Pontifical Throne; "but this assertion has no foundation in law or practice.

3. Besides velvet, the Pope makes use of *silk,* either watered or plain; but, among silk materials, *satin* likewise is exclusively reserved for him. In winter, he lays aside his silk dress, and wears a light one of fine broadcloth. Both in winter and summer, he wears a dress of serge on penitential days. [2]

4. *Watered silk* is reserved for Cardinals. They make use of this rich and beautiful material for the choir-cassock, *cappa magna, mantelletta* and *mozzetta* during the summer season. In winter, the cassock, *mantelletta* and *mozzetta* are of broad cloth. [3]

5. *Plain silk* is the material of which the costumes of the Papal Court and Household are made. [4] In summer, the Prelates *di mantelletta* and the Prelates *di mantellone,* whether they live at the Roman court or outside of the City, must wear a cassock of plain purple silk, and, respectively, a *mantelletta* or a *mantellone* of the same material. Broadcloth replaces silk in winter. [5]

Archbishops and Bishops who have received the title of *Assistants at the Pontifical Throne* belong to the Papal Household and are, therefore, entitled to wear a silk costume, but only when they actually live in Rome. Outside of the papal city, they are not allowed to wear a dress different from that of other Bishops. [6]

6. According to the Ceremonial of Bishops, *broadcloth* and other *woolen materials* only are allowed to be used in making the costumes of the Cardinals who belong to Religious Orders, and of Archbishops, Bishops and Clergy, both secular and regular. For all these Prelates and the secular clergy, etiquette prescribes cloth in winter, and some lighter material, as merino, in summer. [7] The Sovereign Pontiff himself, although, strictly speaking, not bound by any such rules, conforms nevertheless to the principle which forbids the wearing of silk garments by the religious: the etiquette of the papal household, faithfully adhered to, is that, when the Pope belongs to a religious order, he always dresses in woolen materials, excepting however the accessories, as indicated in the following paragraph.

Although Archbishops and Bishops, whether regular or secular, are expected to dress at all times in woolen materials (except, in the case of seculars, if they be Assistants at the Pontifical Throne and actually living in Rome); yet church regulations allow them the use of silk for the accessories of the prelatial dress, such as the *collaro,* skull-cap, biretta, cincture, gloves, stockings and the lining and trimmings of the different garments; but the silk material thus allowed must be *plain;* neither satin nor watered silk is ever permitted, since the former is reserved for the Pope and the latter for secular Cardinals, and velvet is limited to the collar of the winter cloak.

7. There are but two seasons with regard to the wearing of the ecclesiastical dress, *winter* and *summer;* no definite rule however determines the begin ning and the end of these seasons, and it pertains to the Bishop to regulate this for his own diocese, according to the local climatic conditions. In the Northern Hemisphere, the liturgical summer usually begins on Holy Saturday, after the singing of *Alleluia,* and the winter, on All Saints Day.

[1] Barrier de Montault, *Le costume et les usages ecclésiastiques.* Tom. I., p. 53, seq. - There are only two exceptions to that general rule: the first is found in the costume of the trainbearers who wear a purple cassock with buttons and trimmings of black velvet; the second is in the prelatial winter cloak which has a velvet collar of the same color as the material of the cloak (Cfr. Chapter V., n. 6).

[2] Barbier de Montault, *loc. cit.* - Battandier, *Annuaire Pontifical* (1902), p. 104. - Grimaldi, *op. cit.,* ch. I., p. 6, seq. - Baron Geramb, *Visit to Rome,* pp. 98-104.

[3] Barbier de Montault, op. cit., Tom. I., p. 54. - Grimaldi, *op. cit.,* ch. V., p. 60.

[4] Same references.

[5] Same references.

[6] Barbier de Montault, *ibid.* Grimaldi, *op. cit.,* ch. V., pp. 61 , 62. This privilege is granted to secular prelates only, Archbishops and Bishops belonging to religious orders should never wear silk clothes.

[7] Caer. *Episc.* L, i., 1. I., in., 1. Benedict XIII., Const. *Custodes* (March 7, 1725). Un Évêque Suffragant, *Le Cérémonial des Évêques commenté et expliqué.* Liv. I., Ch. I., p. 2.

Chapter Three - Colors

1. The colors adopted for the ecclesiastical costume are: *White, Red, Purple* and *Black.* To these colors proper for the secular clergy, must be added the different colors prescribed for the Religious Orders by their respective Constitutions [1] and the decrees of the Sacred Congregation of the Ceremonial.

2. We have previously remarked that when a member of some Religious Order is promoted to the Cardinalate or the episcopal dignity, he must retain, for his prelatical costume, the color used for the habit of the Order to which he belongs. However, he may adopt a finer material and the shape of the costume of secular Prelates. We speak here of the Religious Orders properly so-called only, as Benedictines, Carmelites, Franciscans, Dominicans, Augustinians, etc. The *Clerics Regular,* as Jesuits, Redemptorists, Passionists, etc., when promoted to prelatical rank, adopt for their costume that of secular Prelates, without, however, being allowed to use silk, except for the cincture, skullcap, biretta and other small accessories. [2]

3. Since the seventeenth century, *black* is the obligatory color for the clothing of the secular clergy of second rank in all the Western Church. [3] There is no exception to this general regulation, save for the clergy of tropical countries, who are permitted to wear white clothes on account of the exceedingly hot climate; and for seminarians and members of the Bishop's household, who should wear a purple cassock.

Prelates, Bishops and the members of the Sacred College also use black [4] for their everyday costume (and their street-dress in Catholic countries); but *their black dress is trimmed with red or purple,* according to their rank in the hierarchy, and the different seasons of the ecclesiastical year, as will be explained further on.

4. *Purple,* or *violet,* is a sign both of Prelature and of Livery. It especially characterizes the Prelature and the Episcopacy; but as it is an official dress, it can be worn only in church functions and on certain well defined occasions.

Purple is the proper color to be used by Cardinals in times of penance and mourning, while Bishops should, at such times, make use of black only. The general rule holds good, that when Cardinals exchange their red costume for purple, Bishops exchange their purple for black. [5]

5. It is an error to suppose that a purple cassock is exclusively a prelatical privilege. It is likewise the color reserved for *ecclesiastical Livery.*

First of all, it is the color used by the whole Pontifical Household. [6] With the exception of the *Bussolanti,* who are clad in red, all others, no matter what their rank, dignity or employment at the Papal Court, Prelates, ushers of the palace, chanters, clerics, acolytes of the Papal chapel, chamber valets, etc., all wear purple as a distinctive sign of their rank, dignity or office. [7]

Secondly, purple is the color of the episcopal Livery. Thus, according to rules laid down by the Ceremonials, [8] the Master of Ceremonies of the cathedral church, the train-bearer of the Bishop, [9] the cross-bearer of the Metropolitan, [10] all the members of the diocesan Seminary, as well as the employees of the cathedral, namely, sacristans, ushers, chanters, etc., all should wear purple cassocks.

However, the use of purple for the collaro, sash and stockings, is an exclusive prelatial privilege, and the purple skull-cap and purple biretta are exclusive episcopal insignia. Therefore, those who may wear a purple cassock as a livery costume are never allowed to wear a purple collaro, or purple stockings, much less a purple skull-cap or a purple biretta.

6. *White* is reserved for the Pope. He uses it for his cassock, simar and other ordinary clothing. But he uses red for his cloak, mozzetta, hat and shoes. [11]

7. *Scarlet red* is proper for Cardinals. [12]

8. Bishops and the Prelates *di mantelletta* may use *amaranth red* [13] for the trimmings of their black dress, such as buttons, buttonholes, lining, etc. The trimmings of their purple dress are of crimson red. At all times, the same accessories must be purple in the dress of the Prelates *di mantellone;* and, for Bishops, in penitential seasons and on occasions of mourning.

9. *Other colors* that may be met with in some places are worn through special privileges granted by the Sovereign Pontiff, or by virtue of immemorial customs having the force of law.

[1] Benedict XIII., *Const. cit.* - Ferraris, *Bibliotheca,* art. *Episcopus.*
[2] *Caer. Episc.,* I.,i.,4.
[3] Decree of Pope Urban VIII (Novem. 26, 1624).
[4] Cf. Un Évêque Suffragant, *Cérémonial des Évêques commenté et expliqué,* p 13.
[5] Barbier de Montault, *op. cit.,* Tom. I., p. 58.
[6] Grimaldi, *Les congrégations romaines,* ch. V.
[7] Barbier de Montault, *op. cit.,* Tom. I., p. 58.
[8] *Caer. Episc.* I., V., 4. S. R. C, February 29, 1868. Dec. 14, 1894.
[9] Levavasseur-Haegy, *Fonctions Pontificales,* II., p. 273. - S. R. C., Aug. 2, 1608. - Jan. 24, 1660.
[10] Levavasseur-Haegy, *Fonctions Pontificales,* II., p. 305.
[11] All Ceremonials *in loco.* - Barbier de Montault, *op. cit.,* Tom. I., p. 57. Baron Geramb, *Visit to Rome,* Letter X., pp. 98-104. - Fisquet, *Ceremonies de Rome* (passim).
[12] Decree of Innocent IV. (1244). - Decree of Boniface VIII (1248). - Barbosa, *Iuris eccles. univ.,* Lib. I., Cap. III., n. 8.
[13] *Amaranth red* is a color inclining to purple.

Part II - Different Parts of the Prelatial Costume

In this Second Part, all the different pieces of the prelatical dress will be studied successively, each one furnishing the subject of a short and substantial chapter.

Chapter One - Cassock or Soutane

The *Cassock* (or *Soutane, Vestis, Vestis talaris, Subtanna, Subtanea*) is the principal part of the ecclesiastical costume. It is a long, close garment covering the entire body from the neck to the feet, hence its Latin name, *Vestis talaris,* a garment reaching to the heels. [1]

All the decrees of Councils, legislating upon ecclesiastical attire, prescribe that the cassock is to be worn by all clerics in sacred Orders in the place of their residence. [2]

The decree of the Third Plenary Council of Baltimore is as follows: "...*Volumus itaque et praecipimus ut omnes Ecclesiae legem servent, domique agentes vel in templo, veste talari quae clerico propria est, semper utantur.*" III., 77. [3]

The obligation of wearing the cassock is the same for Prelates, Priests and other clerics; [4] but here we treat only of the cassock as worn by Prelates, and we distinguish two kinds of prelatial cassocks:
1. The *ordinary* or every-day *cassock.*
2. The *choir cassock.*

Article I - Ordinary Cassock

1. The ordinary cassock is that worn by Prelates in daily life, at home and in church, at private ceremonies, such as the celebration of Low Mass. In Catholic countries, it is worn out of doors.

This cassock should not be mistaken for the "simar," which will be dealt with in the following chapter.

The model of the ordinary cassock, according to Roman etiquette, is the same as that universally adopted in this country. It must be noted, how ever, that the front part should be made of only one piece dropping from the neck to the feet, [5] and not of two pieces (waist and skirt) sewed together, as is often done.

The sleeves are wide, and are turned up with plain cuffs without buttons.

From the neck to the feet, the front part is fastened with a row of small round buttons covered with silk.

The collar (a standing collar) is cut out square in front, in order to show the Roman collar.

This cassock has no train; its bottom is cut round, the front and the back being of equal length. The train is the distinctive characteristic of the choir cassock. [6]

The garment has two pockets, one on each side. Interior pockets may be added at will, but there should be no exterior pocket for the watch, Roman etiquette forbidding any metallic ornament other than the chain of the pectoral cross. The watch may be put in the pocket of the vest, or in a special pocket on the inside of the cassock.

The ordinary cassock varies in color, according to the different degrees of the ecclesiastical hierarchy.

2. The Pope's ordinary cassock is entirely white, without trimmings of any color. The material for this cassock is brilliant silk satin, in summer, and fine broadcloth in winter. White watered silk is ordinarily reserved for his choir cassock. [7]

3. The ordinary cassock of Cardinals is made of black woolen material lined and trimmed with scarlet red silk. [8]

4. Archbishops, Bishops, and the Prelates *di mantelletta* wear the same ordinary cassock as the Cardinals; except that the trimmings and lining are of amaranth red silk, instead of scarlet. [9]

5. The Prelates *di mantellone* wear also the same style of cassock, but with purple trimmings and lining. [10]

6. Some Canons (for instance, those of Montreal, Canada,) are allowed a special cassock with red or purple trimmings (purple for those of Montreal); but this cassock should never be worn outside the limits of the diocese in which the Chapter is constituted, except when accompanying their Bishop or representing him or the chapter at councils or other solemnities. [11]

7. Religious, when promoted to the Cardinalate or to the episcopal dignity, lay aside the habit of the Order and wear the cassock; but for them there is no difference of color between the ordinary cassock and the choir cassock; both cassocks are of the same color as the habit of the Order, as was said in the preceding chapter. [12]

8. Cardinals and Bishops taken from Religious Congregations or Orders of Clerics Regular follow, as regards their ordinary cassocks, the rules laid down for Prelates belonging to the secular clergy.

Before closing this article, and in answer to several queries which have come to the author, it may be useful to remark that Cardinals, Archbishops, Bishops and other Prelates belonging to the secular clergy or to congregations of Clerics Regular are not obliged to wear at all times the black cassock with red or purple trimmings at home, in private, they are permitted to wear an ordinary black cassock like that of a simple priest.

Article II. Choir Cassock

1. The choir cassock is so called because it is worn by Prelates in choir, [13] at the public ceremonies of the Church. It may be worn also on some certain

specified occasions when a Prelate is called upon to vest in his choir habit. It is also called "church cassock", because it is worn chiefly in church and at church functions.

2. The shape of the choir cassock, according to Roman etiquette, is almost the same as that of the ordinary cassock. The only exception is that the choir cassock has a tram, which may be let down on occasions determined by the Ceremonial. [14]

The materials and colors of choir cassocks differ, and thus mark the different degrees in the ecclesiastical hierarchy.

3. The Pope, whenever he has to appear in his choir habit, puts on a cassock of white watered silk, over which, for ecclesiastical functions, "chapels," consistories, he puts the *falda,* a kind of large skirt of the same color and material. [15]

4. The choir cassock of the Cardinals is scarlet red at ordinary times; purple in penitential seasons, and on occasions of mourning, like the vacancy of the Holy See or when they attend a funeral; and rose-colored on the third Sunday of Advent (*Gaudete*) and the fourth Sunday of Lent (*Laetare*). [16]

Both the red and purple cassocks must be made of watered silk for summer, and of fine broadcloth for winter. The rose-colored cassock is always of watered silk, though both Sundays on which it is worn usually occur during the liturgical winter. [17]

5. As is well known, the ordinary choir cassock of a Bishop is purple, with lining, cuffs and trimmings of crimson red silk. 2 But the cassock itself must be exclusively made of woolen material, as cloth in winter and merino in summer, 3 unless the Bishop has received the title of Assistant at the Pontifical Throne, and is actually living in Rome. The purple cassock is a festival or court dress and is to be worn on occasions indicated in the first book, chapter III, of

Choir Cassock of a Prelate with the tram lifted up

the Ceremonial of Bishops. [20] At other times, and principally on ferial days, penitential seasons, funerals, times of public mourning, vacancy of the Holy See, etc., Archbishops and Bishops must wear a choir cassock of black material lined and trimmed in purple. This black cassock is of course different from the every-day cassock mentioned and described in the preceding article: it is a choir cassock, and therefore is cut exactly like the purple cassock, has no cape or double sleeves, ends in a train at the back, and its trimmings are not red but purple. As will be seen further on, this black choir cassock is completed by a *mozetta* and a *mantelletta* of the same colors and materials.

But the wearing of this black choir cassock is a sort of privilege of Archbishops and Bishops which is not entirely shared by the Domestic Prelates; There are no ferial days for the Pontifical House hold, except Good Friday and the vacancy of the Holy See; therefore Archbishops and Bishops, when actually living in Rome, must wear the purple cassock, regardless of the paragraph of the Ceremonial of Bishops just alluded to. The only occasions on which they wear the black choir cassock in Rome, are upon the vacancy of the Holy See, and on Good Friday.

6. All the regulations concerning the wearing of the choir cassock by Bishops apply to the Prelates *di mantelletta;* but, both in Rome and else where, these Prelates always rank as members of the Pontifical Court and Household, and must every where follow its etiquette, that is, wear a purple choir cassock of silk in summer, and of fine broad cloth in winter, trimmed, like that of Bishops, with crimson red silk, without regard to the liturgical season; these Prelates being forbidden to wear mourning, except at the Pope's death, until the election of his successor, and on Good Friday. [21]

7. The Prelates *di mantellone* do not wear mourning at the Pope's death; because they are appointed for his lifetime only and lose their Prelacy at his death. Nor do they wear the penitential costume, for they belong to the Papal Court. Therefore, they make use of only one choir cassock of purple silk in summer, and of purple cloth in winter, as is prescribed for all members of the Pontifical Household. But their cassock differs from that of Bishops and of the Prelates di mantelletta inasmuch as it is without train, and is not trimmed with red, but with purple silk of a lighter hue than that of the cassock. [22]

8. Certain Chapters enjoy the privilege of wearing in choir a red or purple cassock. When such a privilege is granted by the Sovereign Pontiff, precise regulations accompany the indult of concession as to the material, shape and color of the cassock, and the occasions on which it is to be used. It is the duty of the Ordinary to care for the exact observance of these prescriptions.

9. The purple cassock, which is worn as a livery garment, is made like that of the Prelates *di mantellone.* It has no train, and is trimmed with purple of a lighter hue.

10. Religious promoted to episcopal dignity or to the Cardinalate wear a choir cassock shaped like that of secular Bishops and Cardinals, but of the same color as the habit of the Order to which they belong; the cassock of the

Franciscans being ash-colored gray, as already said. Members of religious Congregations, or Clerics Regular, vest like secular Prelates, with the usual restrictions as to the wearing of silk.

[1] Rubric of the Missal, *Rit. serv. in celeb. Miss.*, n. 2.

[2] Council of Trent, Sess. XIV., Cap. VI., de *Reform*.

[3] "...We wish, therefore, and we command that all [ecclesiastics] keep the Law of the Church, and, whether at home or in church, always wear the cassock, which is the proper garb for clerics."

[4] Council of Trent., Sess. XIV., *Decret de Reform. Proaemium*.

[5] Barbier de Montault, *op. cit*, Tom. I., p. 78, seq.

[6] Barbier de Montault, *loc. cit.* - Grimaldi, *op. cit.*, p. 53.

[7] Grimaldi, *op. cit.*, Ch. I. Barbier de Montault, *op. cit.*, Tom. I., p. 275. - Baron Geramb, *Visit to Rome*, Letter X. - J. de Narfon, *Léon XIII. intime*, p. 136.

[8] Un Évêque Suffragant, *op. cit.*, p. 13. - Barbier de Montault, *op. cit.*, Tom. I., p. 84. We may remark here, once for all, that the *trimmings* of the prelatical dress consist of a number of small ornaments, the color of which is ordinarily different from that of the principal parts of the costume. These are buttons, buttonholes, pipings, stitchings, cuffs ant two small strips or strings, on the back of the cassock, destined to support the sash. The lining of the garment is of the same color as the trimmings, and of the same material, plain silk.

[9] Pius X., Constit. *Inter multiplices* (1905), nn. 16, 17.

[10] Pius X., same Constit., n. 79.

[11] Codex Juris Canonici, 409, § 2.

[12] *Caer. Episc.* I., I., 4. Cap. *Clerici*, 15. de vita et honest, clericorum. - Ferraris, *Bibliotheca*, Art. *Episcopus*, VII.

[13] The *choir* is the part of the church where the clergy seat when assisting at some church ceremony.

[14] Barbier de Montault, *op. cit.*, Tom. I., p. 275. - It may not be useless to note here that the choir cassock has no cape attached nor double sleeves, as has the "simar" described in the following chapter.

[15] H. Fisquet, *Cérémonies de Rome*, pp. 35, 44, 55, 191, 200... - Barbier de Montault, *op. cit.*, Tom. I., p. 275. - Un Évêque Suffragant, *op. cit.*, p. 274. - Lerosey (édition 1902, revised by A. Vigourel, S. S.), *Abrégé du Manuel Liturgique*, Part V., ch. V., p. 602.

[16] Ferraris, *Bibliotheca*, Art. *Cardinales*.

[17] Barbier de Montault, *op. cit.*, Tom. I., p. 275.

[18] *Caer Episc.* I., III., 1.

[19] *Caer Episc.* I., I., 1.

[20] "...Videlicet a die Nativitatis Domini et per totam Octavam Epiphoniae, a die dominica Resurrectionis usque ad dominicam SS. Trinitatis: item per Octavas festorum SS. Sacramenti, Assumptionis gloriosae Virginis Mariae et beatorum Apostolorum Petri et Pauli, et Omnium Sanctorum, Titularis Ecclesiae Cathedralis et Sancti Patroni civitatis, ac Dedicationis propriae Ecclesiae; item in anniversaries electionis ipsius Episcopi; die adventus alicuius magni Principis, vel cum celebratur aliqua publica laetitia; in aliis vero Octavis, ut Nativitatis gloriosae Virginis, S. Ioannis Baptistae, S. Laurentii, dies tantum Octavarum excipiuntur: similiter omnia festa duplicia, quae per annum incidunt extra Adventum, Septuagesiman et Quadragesimum, sed Annuntiationis festo, etiamsi*

infra Quadragesimam occurrat, vestibus violaceis uti debet. (Caer. Episc. I., III., 2.)
[21] Barbier de Montault, *op. cit.*, Tom. I., p. 276.

[22] *Ibid.* - S. R. C, June 17, 1673. - March 30, 1675. - Sept. 12, 1840. - July 21, 1855.

Chapter Two - Simar

1. Encyclopedias are generally very incomplete, often inexact, in their articles on the Catholic Church. Since the sixteenth century, the English tongue has been mainly Protestant. Hence, the necessity of recurring to foreign or improper terms when we wish to speak of certain things pertaining to the Liturgy of the Church.

We see this exemplified in the case of the ecclesiastical garment of which we are treating in this Chapter. For lack of a proper English word, the terms *cassock* and *zimarra* have been adopted by ecclesiastics and tailors. The former designation (cassock or "home-cassock") is not exact, this garment being somewhat different from the cassock properly so-called. The word "zimarra" is the Italian name of this garment, and has the same etymology and all the different meanings of the English word *simar*. So let us take at least this opportunity of doing away with an improper and a foreign word, and of adopting the English word *simar*, with its Catholic meaning of an ecclesiastical vestment resembling the cassock, but differing from it in that it is adorned with short, buttoned false sleeves and a small unclosed cape adhering to the collar.

2. Strictly speaking, the "simar" should be "a house garment, a kind of ecclesiastical lounging gown. However, during the nineteenth century, it became customary to wear it outside the house, and, as it has been found convenient on account of the extra covering it affords to the shoulders, it has now a tendency to supersede the ordinary cassock for home wear, as also, in Catholic countries, for street wear; and Pius IX. gave it an additional vogue when, after 1870, he allowed its use for private audiences at the Vatican.

Strict propriety however should forbid the use of the simar in church at public functions, for church services ordinarily require the wearing of the surplice or rochet which are to be worn only over the cassock; and it should go without saying that a Prelate must never wear over his black simar a rochet and a purple *mozzetta* or *mantelletta,* for such a combination of discrepant garments might be regarded as an evidence of carelessness.

3. The shape of the simar is approximately the same as that of the ordinary cassock, but differs from it by a small unbuttoned cape attached to the collar and additional short sleeves encasing the long ones, reaching from the shoulders to a little above the elbows, split in front from the soulder down, and fastened with a row of buttons. Like the ordinary cassock, the simar is cut round at the back and does not admit of a train; and for all, except the Pope and the Religious, it is made of black woolen material, with red or purple trimmings according to the season and the rank of the wearer.

Pope wearing the Simar

4. The Pope's simar is entirely white, of satin in summer, and fine broad-cloth for winter wear. It is cut like the simar of the other classes of Prelates and needs no special description; the many portraits of the recent Pontiffs have made this papal garment familiar even to people who have never had an audience with the Pope.

The Cardinals simar is black with scarlet trimmings; and a similar black simar trimmed with amaranth red is worn by Archbishops, Bishops and Domestic Prelates; however, on penitential and ferial days reduced for the Domestic Prelates to Good Friday and the vacancy of the Holy See they should wear a black simar trimmed in purple.

This latter style of simar, black with purple trimmings, is that worn at all times by the Prelates *di mantellone*.

5. Among the Prelates belonging to religious orders, the Clerics Regular conform as usual to the rules laid down for the secular Prelates, while the members of the great orders wear the simar of the same colors as the ordinary cassock; but, owing to the fact that the light colored simars, like those of the Dominican or Franciscan Prelates, soil too easily, many of those Prelates now wear in private a black simar trimmed with the distinctive color of the religious habit, white for the Dominicans, light grey for the Franciscans, etc., and reserve the formal religious simar for public occasions.

6. Certain clerical dignitaries are entitled to wear an entirely black simar as an external sign of extended jurisdiction or authority: such are the Vicars General, the Administrators of vacant dioceses, the irremovable parish priests and the Rec tors of Seminaries. It is of course understood that if these dignitaries happen to be Prelates otherwise, they should wear the simar trimmed with red or purple, according to their respective rank in the Prelature.

7. Removable rectors, professors of Seminaries, curates and other priests are by no means entitled to wear the simar, and although clerical tailors advertise the black simar under the name of "Doctor's Cassock", the possession of the Doctorate does not confer the right to wear that distinguished garment.

Chapter Three - Roman Collar

1. Ecclesiastics who have lived or studied in Rome may have noticed that what we usually call a Roman Collar is a collar indeed, but not Roman, except, as will be said later, by adoption.

Our Roman Collar, so-called, consists of two parts, a starched circle of white linen the collar, and a piece of cloth or silk, to which the collar itself is fastened by means of buttons or hooks, a sort of stock which has been given the somewhat strange name of "rabbi" probably a corruption of the French word "rabat".

Now, it may be a surprise to many, but it is none the less true, that what is familiar to us under the name of "rabbi" is the true *Roman collar,* called in Rome *collaro.*

The Roman *collaro* is made up of a loose breastpiece and of a rigid circle of the same material. The rigid part is properly the collar, and is maintained stiff by slipping into it a piece of light cardboard or leather. In order to keep the collar clean, a changeable band of white linen (*collarino*) is placed over it and fixed behind with two silver clips. It is that small band of linen which has grown into the stiff affair now worn, and has usurped among us the name of "Roman collar."

And so well has it succeeded in its usurpation, that it has been adopted almost universally, not only in this country, but elsewhere, and even in Italy, as the new form of the Roman collar. In Rome now nobody objects to its use.

And if we consider that this new form of the "Roman collar" renders it easier to wear as a part of the civilian dress of ecclesiastics, we have every reason not to change what may be regarded as the universal custom on this point. The only change that might be suggested to ecclesiastics and tailors would be to do away with that peculiar Jewish word "rabbi", which is certainly out of place here, and could be advantageously replaced by the Italian word *collaro*. [1]

2. Though treating exclusively of the prelatial costume, it may not be useless to remark here that the *collaro*, for priests and for other members of the inferior clergy, must be made entirely of woolen material, silk being reserved for the *collaro* of Prelates and of such dignitaries as have received a special indult to that effect. A *fortiori* velvet is never allowed, nor even conceded.

Therefore, good sisters and pious ladies who, at Christmas time, overwhelm priests and seminarians with gifts of "rabbis," should take notice of this rule and offer only woolen *collari*.

3. The *collaro* is essentially a sign of Prelacy, when it is made in another color than black. [2] Those who wear the red or purple cassock by privilege or custom, without being Prelates, should never wear a red or purple *collaro*, unless it is expressly granted by an Apostolic indult. The same rule applies to all who wear a purple cassock as a livery dress.

4. The Pope's *collaro* is white, like the main parts of his official dress. That of the Cardinals is scarlet; of Bishops and other Prelates, purple. [3] When a Chapter have received the privilege of wearing red or purple *collari*, they are not allowed to wear them outside the limits of their diocese, [4] except in cases mentioned by the Code of Canon Law, canon 409, §2.

[1] The *"single band Roman collar,"* which seems to be in favor in some parts of the country, and is advertised as a "specialty" by certain clerical tailors, should be left to the clergymen of the "Episcopal Church."

[2] Cong, of Bps. and Reg., 1848. Amalphitan. Gregory XVI.'s Brief, *Ecclesiasticos viros,* Nov. 17, 1843.

[3] Religious Prelates should wear a *collaro* of the same color as the cassock.

[4] Decrees quoted above.

Chapter Four - Cincture

1. There are two kinds of prelatial cinctures, one used in ordinary life, the other reserved for church ceremonies and whenever the choir habit is worn; the former, about five inches wide, is properly adorned with fringes at both ends; the latter, usually a little wider, terminates in tassels or tufts; both are exclusively made of silk, but, according to general principles, the cinctures of the Pope and Cardinals are made of watered silk, while the other Prelates should content themselves with cinctures of plain silk. [1]

2. The cincture, belt, or sash (called *fascia* in Ceremonials and other Latin documents), [2] is for the Clergy a sign of jurisdiction, and for Prelates a mark of their dignity.

The cincture may be worn over the cassock or over the simar. But there is no obligation to wear it at home in private. The Prelate wears it at home only on extraordinary occasions, for instance, when receiving formal visits, etc.

3. The Pope, at all times, whether in home dress or in choir habit, wears a cincture of white watered silk with gold fringes or tassels.

Cardinals wear, over the ordinary black cassock or over the simar, a red cincture of watered silk adorned with red fringes or tassels. The cincture which they use with the choir cassock matches the color of the cassock, red, purple, or rose-colored, but always has gold tassels at the ends, this being the special privilege of the Pope and Cardinals.

At ordinary times, Bishops and the Prelates *di mantelletta* are entitled to wear a purple cincture of plain silk over the choir cassock, the ordinary black cassock and the simar. When they wear mourning (black cassock with purple trimmings), they put on a cincture of plain black silk with fringes or tufts of the same color. [3] The cincture of the Prelates *di mantellone* is of no other color than purple.

4. Irremovable parish priests, as a sign of ordinary jurisdiction, and Rectors of Seminaries as a sign of authority, are privileged to wear a black cincture of plain silk with fringes at the bottom.

5. Cardinals and Bishops belonging to Religious Orders make use of a cincture, the color of which matches that of the cassock, unless special regulations or the traditions of the Order are in opposition to this general rule, as is the case for the Carmelite Cardinals, who wear a purple cincture. Whatever be the color of the cincture, its material is silk, the cincture being one of the accessories of the costume, in which silk is permitted to Religious Prelates.

6. The cincture is conceded by special favor to some Chapters. But in this case as in that of all other insignia granted to Chapters, the express terms of the concession must be observed strictly, and, unless determined otherwise, the use of the cincture is not permitted outside the limits of the diocese, except in cases mentioned in Canon 409, §2.

7. All who wear a purple cassock as a sign of Livery or domesticity, should wear also a purple cincture. The only exception is in the case of Seminarians, [4] because these wear over their purple cassock an upper garment called *soprana,* much like the *mantellone.*

8. Altar boys who, in liturgical functions, are permitted to perform the duties of clerics must wear the cassock and the surplice; but the Sacred Congregation of Rites forbids them to wear a cincture. [5]

[1] Barbier de Montault, *op. cit.,* Tom. I., pp. 91, seq., 285, 286.
[2] Cfr. for inst. Pius X.'s *motu proprio "Inter multiplices,"* given in Appendix.
[3] Barbier de Montault, *op. cit.,* Tom. I., p. 285.
[4] *Caer. Episc.* I., v., 2, 3. - S. R. C, April 3, 1900.

Chapter Five - Cloak

1. The Roman cloak, which is given, by our clerical tailors, its Italian name of *ferraiolo* or *ferraiolone*, [1] is the necessary complement of the ecclesiastical habit, and is worn by all members of the clergy.

In this country, it would be proper to wear it on solemn occasions, when the full clerical costume is required and admitted, for instance, at banquets, entertainments, receptions of distinguished guests, academic solemnities, and the like.

The Roman cloak is required also for the priest or Prelate who delivers a funeral oration; [2] for the judges of the episcopal court [3] and the examiners of the clergy, whenever they discharge the duties of their office.

Priests and Prelates acting as mourners at a funeral take their place in the procession in the mourners rank, wearing the Roman cloak.

The Chaplains (*Familiares*) of the Bishop, at Pontifical Mass and other so lemn services, should serve in black cassock and cloak, not in surplice. [4]

2. The cloak must be made of light material. It is very large, so that it falls in graceful folds about the body from the shoulders to the feet. At the neck, it is tied with two ribbons, and a large stiff collar folding back over the shoulders gives a complete finish to the garment. The cloak should have no lining, except at the collar.

Priest wearing the Cloak (ferraiolo).

3. The cloak of simple priests and other members of the inferior clergy, is always black and made of light woolen material.

4. The Prelates *di mantellone,* on all official occasions when they do not vest in the purple cassock, should wear a cloak (*ferraiolone*) of plain black silk.

35

Patriarchs, Archbishops, Bishops and Prelates *di mantelletta* wear the *ferraiolone* of purple silk as described in paragraph 17 of the Constitution *Inter multiplices,* and tailors must note that the trimmings of this cloak, such as hems, ribbons, stitchings and the lining of the collar, must be of the same purple as the rest of the garment. When these Prelates dress in mourning, as, for instance, when a Bishop delivers a funeral oration, they wear with the penitential cassock a *ferraiolone* of plain black silk like that of the Prelates *di mantellone.* [5]

5. Cardinals have two different cloaks; one, of scarlet watered silk, for ordinary occasions; the other, purple, worn during penitential seasons and in times of mourning. But this purple cloak differs from that of Bishops in that it is made of watered silk and trimmed with plain red silk. [6]

The cloak of Prelates belonging to Religious Orders is of the same color as the outer part of the religious habit, as was indicated in the chapter treating of the cassock. There may be found exceptions to this general rule, for the costume of Religious Prelates is regulated by local traditions rather than by strict etiquette; but the rule given here is that followed at the Roman Court and adopted by nearly all Religious Prelates outside of Rome.

6. In winter, Prelates may wear a large cloak of broadcloth, finished with an attached cape which falls a little below the elbows, and a velvet rolling collar, not more than four inches wide. This style of cloak is familiar enough to our tailors, who generally call it a "confessional cloak". When well made, according to

Priest wearing the Winter Cloak

proper regulations, it is a very comfortable and graceful garment; but tailors often make it too short and narrow and without the cape, while it should be the same length as the cassock, and so ample that, when spread on a large surface, it forms a complete circle. It is not, strictly speaking, an official cloak, but is worn chiefly for comfort.

The cloak worn by the Pope is well-known from pictures of recent Pontiffs. A feature which distinguishes his cloak from that of other Prelates is that it

has a standing, instead of a rolling, collar. The cloak is made of scarlet broad-cloth and is lined in front with red satin. The clasp by which it is fastened in front is made of gold, and the cape is bordered with an entwined cord of gold and red.

For all other clergymen, the winter cloak has the same shape,. It should be made of broadcloth, with a velvet rolling collar, and lined in front with two wide bands of silk; the clasp is of gold for Cardinals, of silver for other Prelates, and of black metal for the rest of the clergy.

For informal wear, the prelatial winter cloak is not different, in material or color, from that of lower clerics; but, for more formal occasions, the cloak worn by Cardinals is of scarlet red; Patriarchs, Archbishops, Bishops and Domestic Prelates wear a purple cloak, and Prelates *di mantellone*, as well as other members of the clergy, wear a black one. In mourning or penitential dress, the Cardinal's cloak is purple, with a red collar and lining, and that of all others is of solid black. At all times, according to the general principles already stated, Prelates belonging to the great Religious Orders wear a winter cloak of the same color as the outer part of their order habit. It should be the same shape as that of the secular Prelates.

Whether religious or secular, all Cardinals and Patriarchs, by right, and Archbishops, by custom, are distinguished by a narrow border of gold braid around the bottom of the cape.

[1] There exists a difference between the *ferraiolo* and the *ferraiolone*. The *ferraiolo* is the cloak which is worn in the streets of Rome and other cities of Catholic countries, while the *ferraiolone,* which is larger and more solemn, is reserved for public occasions. The *ferraiolo* is always black and made of light woolen material, but Prelates do not wear it so much nowadays; when they go out for a walk or an unofficial call, they put on a sort of long double-breasted overcoat known to tailors by its French name of "douillette", which facetious clerics in Rome call *copri-miseria*. - The word *"ferraiolo"* should not be corrupted into *"feriola,"* as is often done in catalogues of clerical tailors.
[2] *Caer. Episc.* I., XXII., 6. - II., XI., 10. Un Évêque Suffragant, *op. cit.*, p. 295.
[3] Unless it is provided otherwise by diocesan statutes.
[4] Caer. *Episc.* I., XI., 2-12. - I., XV., 2. - Levavasseur, *Fonctions Pontificales* (Édition 1904), p. 263.
[5] When a Domestic Prelate delivers a funeral oration, he must wear the purple cloak, for he is not supposed to wear mourning for anybody but the Pope.
[6] Barbier de Montault, *op. cit.*, Tom. I., pp. 107, 108. Grimaldi, *op. cit.* Ch. VIII, p. 113.

Chapter Six - Rochet

1. The rochet is a close-fitting garment of linen, [1] something like a surplice, but with tight sleeves. The opening for the neck may be cut square, like that of the cotta; the bottom, the shoulder-pieces, and the extremities of the

sleeves, ornamented with lace. [2] Under the lace, at the shoulder-pieces and sleeves, is put a silk lining, visible through the lace. This lining is of the same color as the trimmings of the choir cassock, that is, white for the Pope, scarlet for Cardinals, amaranth red for Patriarchs, Archbishops, Bishops and Domestic Prelates. In penitential seasons, and on occasions of mourning, the lining of a Bishop's rochet is purple. [3] On the same occasions, Cardinals do not change the color of the lining of their rochets, because the trimmings of a Cardinal's mourning dress are scarlet.

Canons who have the privilege of wearing the rochet are not regularly entitled to have in the rochet any other lining than black, unless the choir cassock granted them be red or purple, in which case, they are permitted to wear the rochet lining of the same color as the cuffs of their cassock sleeves.

When a Prelate *di mantellone* is granted the use of the rochet a rare case he is allowed in his rochet purple lining only. The rochet of "black Protonotaries" admits of no other lining than black.

The rochet has, on the breast, a vertical slit, which may be bordered with lace, and is tied near the neck with two ribbons of silk, which are not necessarily white but may be of the same color as the lining of the rochet.

A plain rochet without lace is a sign of official mourning; such a rochet is worn by all Prelates residing in Rome from the day of the Pope's death until the election of his successor, and at services on Good Friday. The ordinary rochet must have lace and be tastefully plaited.

2. The uncovered rochet is a sign of Ordinary Jurisdiction. Therefore, the Pope and Cardinals all over the world, Archbishops in their provinces, Bishops in their dioceses, Abbots in their monasteries, alone have the right to wear the rochet uncovered. [4] Practically the rochet is always partly covered with some other vestment. However, a Cardinal at Rome, a Bishop outside of his diocese, and all the Prelates who have the privilege of wearing the rochet without having "ordinary jurisdiction," should entirely cover the rochet with the *mantelletta*. [5] Abbots in their monasteries, Bishops in their dioceses, Archbishops in their provinces, and Cardinals everywhere, except at Rome, wear the *mozzetta* over the rochet. [6]

3. The Ceremonial of Bishops directs that Carclinals and Bishops belonging to religious orders do not wear the rochet, but only the mozzetta, [7] and, for sacred functions, they are supposed to take off the mozzetta and put on the surplice; [8] but this rule, which of course did not apply to Bishops belonging to Orders of Clerics regular or to Religious Congregations, [9] has now fallen into disuse. When a religious is made Cardinal or Bishop, he receives at the same time the privilege of wearing the rochet like secular Prelates; and the same favor is also extended to Abbots. All these Prelates should have the sleeves and shoulder-pieces of their rochets lined with silk material of the same color as the cuffs of the choir cassock which they are privileged to wear.

4. The Pope, Cardinals, Patriarchs, Archbishops, and Bishops have by law the full right to use the rochet. It is the principal part of their choir-habit. The Rubrics of the Missal direct them to keep the rochet on under the alb when they vest for Mass. [10] They may use the rochet for the administration of the sacraments, for the pastoral visitation and for Confirmation given without solemnity. According to the Ceremonial of Bishops, they should also wear the rochet when receiving the Viaticum. [11]

The Protonotaries Apostolic of the first three classes wear the rochet without any other restriction than the obligation to cover it with the *mantelletta*. [12] The same rule holds good for all the Prelates *di mantelletta* who belong to a Prelatial College. The Prelates *di mantelletta*, who do not belong to a college, i.e., those who are simply appointed as Domestic Prelates," formerly were not permitted to wear the rochet in Rome, unless granted that privilege by a personal indult, but this restriction does not obtain any longer; nowadays the privilege of wearing the rochet, *etiam intra Urbem*, is always mentioned in the brief appointing a Domestic Prelate.

The Prelates *di mantellone* are not entitled to wear the rochet, unless they have received a personal indult to do so. At no time are they allowed to wear it in Rome.

Since the *motu proprio* of Pope Pius X. (Feb. 21, 1905), Titular Protonotaries Apostolic have the privilege of wearing the rochet under the black *mantelletta*. But as they are merely diocesan Prelates, they are never allowed to wear their prelatial costume in Rome. [13]

5. The privilege of wearing the rochet is usually granted to cathedral Chapters; but, unless the bull of institution or brief of concession states otherwise, the Canons are forbidden by law (Can. 409, § 2) to wear the rochet outside the diocese, except on the two occasions mentioned in the same canon.

6. When a chapter, as is frequently the case, is granted the privilege of wearing the *cappa magna*, this privilege includes that of wearing the rochet, for the *cappa* and the rochet go together; but, the *cappa magna* being a winter garment, the canons must not wear it in summer time; the cappa then must be substituted by the surplice or cotta which is to be worn over the rochet. [14] In some rare cases however, chapters are granted also the use of a summer *cappa* or cape, which exempts the canons from wearing the surplice or cotta as part of their choir dress; but, in any case, whenever they are called upon to administer the sacraments or perform any other church function requiring the wearing of a stole, they must vest in the rochet and the surplice or cotta before they put on the stole, for no one but the Pope is ever allowed to wear a stole over a "cape", be that "cape" a *cappa magna*, a *mozzetta*, a *mantelletta*, a *mantellone* or any sort of cloak; and only Cardinals and Prelates invested with the episcopal character may wear a stole directly over the rochet. Even Archbishops and Bishops who happen to be in Rome on Holy Thursday and receive holy communion from the Pope must, for that occasion, wear the cotta over the rochet.

[1] *Caer. Episc.* I., I., 2, 3.

[2] Pius IX., Brief *Sacerdotalia indumenta* (May 14, 1858).
[3] The same regulations apply to the albs worn by Prelates when celebrating Mass.
[4] Caer. *Episc.* I., III., 1.
[5] Caer. *Episc.* I., I., 1.I., IV., 7.
[6] Caer. *Episc.* I., I., 1. I., III., 1.
[7] Caer. *Episc.* I., I., 4.
[8] Caer. *Episc.* I., I., 4. - *Rub. Miss.* - S. R. C., Dec. 3, 1701. - *Caer. Episc.* II., XI., 13. - *Pont Rom., de confirm.; de ordin. conf.*
[9] Caer. *Episc.* I., I., 4.
[10] *Rub. Miss.* (*Ritus serv. in cel. Miss.,* n. 2). - *Pont. Rom.* (*passim*).

[11] *Caer. Episc.* II., XXXVIII., 3.
[12] Pius X., Constit. *Inter multiplices* (1905), nn. 3, 16, 45.
[13] Pius X.'s Const. *Inter multiplices* (1905), n. 64. Before the *motu proprio* of Pius X., they had a right to wear the rochet under the *mantelletta,* but in church ceremonies only; now, they have the same right as the other Prelates, to wear the rochet under the *mantelletta* every where and on every occasion, except in Rome, or in any other place where the Pope might actually reside.
[14] *Caer. Episc.* I., III., 3.

Chapter Seven - Mozzetta

1. *Mozzetta* is an Italian word derived from *mozzo,* which means *cut short.* The mozzetta is an ecclesiastical vestment, a short cape, which covers the shoulders, is buttoned over the breast, and to which a small hood is attached. [1]

2. The mozzetta is by itself a sign of jurisdiction. [2] Therefore, it can lawfully be worn only by the Pope, Cardinals and within the limits of their jurisdiction by Archbishops, Bishops and Abbots.

The mozzetta is made of different materials and colors according to the different grades of the Sacred Hierarchy.

3. The Pope's jurisdiction being unlimited, he may wear the mozzetta everywhere throughout the world. His mozzetta is of crimson red velvet bordered with ermine. [3] In summer, the velvet mozzetta is replaced by one of red silk and without fur. In penitential seasons, the Pope lays aside velvet and silk, and wears a mozzetta of broadcloth or serge. From Holy Saturday until the Saturday after Easter, his mozzetta is of white silk damask. [4]

The Pope has the exclusive privilege of wearing a stole over his mozzetta; that stole is at all times red, except during the octave of Easter, when he wears a white one: red and white, it must be remembered, are the only two colors of the Pope's sacred vestments.

4. The Cardinals, as counsellors of the Holy See, participate in the Pope's universal jurisdiction, and therefore wear the mozzetta everywhere. The color of a Cardinal's mozzetta always matches that of his church cassock, that is, scarlet at ordinary times; purple, lined and trimmed in red, on penitential days and at funeral ceremonies, and rose-colored on the third Sunday of Advent (*Gaudete*) and the fourth Sunday of Lent (*Laetare*). Likewise the material varies with the liturgical seasons, according to the principles stated in the

chapter on the cassock; it is watered silk in the summer and on the two "pink Sundays", and broad cloth in winter time.

5. Bishops should wear a mozzetta of woolen material (broadcloth in winter and merino in summer), silk never being permitted. [5] It is true Bishops who are Assistants at the Pontifical Throne are permitted to wear a costume of silk, but only when they actually live in Rome, and then, they do not wear the mozzetta. [6]

The color of a Bishop's mozzetta must match that of the choir cassock. It is, therefore, purple, [7] except during penitential seasons and on days of mourning, when it is, like the cassock, black with purple stitchings, buttons, buttonholes and lining. The Bishop's purple mozzetta is lined and trimmed with crimson red silk. [8]

As a rule, the mozzetta being a sign of jurisdiction, a Bishop is allowed to wear it only within the limits of his own diocese. [9] The Ceremonial of Bishops (Book I. Ch. III.) briefly indicates some occasions on which a Bishop may wear his mozzetta, namely, when he presides over a religious meeting, for the examination of candidates for

Mozzetta

Orders, and the like. He may wear it when assisting at religious services celebrated without solemnity; but in such case he should not sit upon his throne; the Ceremonial directs that the Ordinary vested in the mozzetta should sit in the first stall of the choir. Of late years, there has been some toleration in this respect, principally in favor of Bishops of poor missionary dioceses whose resources are too small to allow the purchase of a *cappa magna;* but a Bishop in normal circumstances should make it a rule for himself never to appear simply vested in the mozzetta when presiding over important religious ceremonies in his diocese; for such occasions, the proper attire includes the *cappa magna.* When Bishops attend a provincial council, they wear the mozzetta as if they were in their own dioceses, because all the members of the council are looked upon as exercising episcopal jurisdiction *per modum unius* over the whole province. [10]

When a priest receives the official news of his appointment to an episcopal see, should he actually be in the territory of the diocese to which he is appointed Bishop, he is allowed immediately the use of the mozzetta over the rochet. [11] If he is not within the limits of his diocese, he wears the mantelletta over the rochet. [12]

Cardinals, Archbishops and Bishops belonging to the great Religious Orders wear a mozzetta of woolen material usually of the same color as the outer part of the Order habit, the silk lining and trimmings of the mozzetta being determined by decrees of the Sacred Congregation of the Ceremonial and the traditions of the Order. [13]

6. Abbots, in the places where they have jurisdiction, may wear a mozzetta, the color of which conforms to that of their religious habit.

7. In presence of a Cardinal, a Bishop in his diocese and an Archbishop within his province must wear the *mantelletta* and the mozzetta; but if the Cardinal is a Legate *a latere*, they are permitted to wear only the mantelletta over the rochet. [14] Cardinals are the only Prelates in whose presence the Ordinary conceals his rochet; in presence of his Metropolitan, of a Nuncio or a Delegate Apostolic, he does not change his customary dress. [15]

8. In Rome, through respect for the presence of the Sovereign Pontiff, Cardinals wear the rochet covered with the mantelletta, and the mozzetta over the mantelletta; but in their titles, and outside of Rome, they wear the mozzetta immediately over the rochet.

Residential Patriarchs, when outside the bound aries of their Patriarchates, and Titular Patriarchs, wear, as the distinctive sign of their high dignity, the mozzetta over the mantelletta. [16] This style of dress in permitted also to Archbishops and Bishops outside of their respective jurisdictions, if there is an established custom to that effect; this custom is rare and does not obtain in the United States, but our Bishops may of course follow it when travel ling in countries where it exists. [17]

9. Many cathedral and collegiate Chapters enjoy, by special favor of the Holy See, the privilege of the mozzetta. This canonical mozzetta may have a peculiar shape and color, or be of the same style as that of Bishops; but, whatever be the case, Canons are not allowed to wear the mozzetta outside the diocese in which the Chapter is constituted, except in the two cases provided by canon 409, § 2, namely, when they escort their Bishop or officially represent the Bishop or the Chapter at councils or other solemnities.

---

[1] This small hood is a vestige of a larger one which was still in use, in some places, in the eighteenth century.
[2] *Caer. Episc.* I., I., 1.
[3] Baron Geramb, *Visit to Rome*, p. 104, and others. - In summer Pius IX. used to wear a mozzetta of red silk, bordered with eiderdown.

[4] Fisquet, *Cérémonies de Rome*, p. 37, and *passim*. A. Battandier, *Annuaire Pontifical* (1901), p. 77.
[5] *Caer. Episc.* I., III., 1.
[6] The only Prelates entitled to wear a purple silk mozzetta are the Patriarchs, as the mozzetta is an integrant part of the costume they wear in Rome; they

are *ex officio* Assistants at the Pontifical Throne, and, therefore, wear a mozzetta of the same material as the other parts of their costume of Assistants.

[7] *Caer Episc., ibid.*
[8] S.R.C., April 17, 1827.
[9] *Caer. Episc.* I., i., 3. S. R. C, Sept. 6, 1895.
[10] *Caer. Episc.* I., III., 1.
[11] *Caer. Episc.*, I., I., 3.
[12] *Caer. Episc.* I., I., 1. - In both cases, he abstains from wearing the pectoral cross and the ring before his consecration.
[13] Martinucci, *Manuale S. Caerem.*, Lib. V., cap. II.
[14] *Caer. Episc.* I., iv., 7. - S. R. C, 1663. - *Caer. Episc.* I., i., 4. - S.R.C.. Sept. 18, 1666.
[15] *Caer. Episc.* I., IV., 7.
[16] Barbier de Montault, *op. cit.*, T. I., p. 335. - A. Battandier, *Annuaire Pontifical* (1898), pp. 66-69. Grimaldi, *op. cit.*, ch. IX., p. 131. - It is understood that, when they are within the limits of their jurisdiction, they wear the mozzetta directly over the rochet, like other Bishops.
[17] *Caer. Episc.* I., i., 4.

Chapter Eight - Mantelletta

1. The *mantelletta* (that is *short mantle*), is a sleeveless garment of silk or woolen material, reaching almost to the knees, used by Prelates to cover the rochet. The mantelletta is open in front and fastened at the neck with a hook, and its collar fits round the collar of the cassock; two vertical slits permit the insertion of the arms. When spread, it forms a complete circle. The trimmings of the mantelletta (lining, stitchings, etc.) are all of silk, and a strip of silk braid should be sewed around the armholes, to prevent them from tearing.

2. The mantelletta is a symbol of restricted jurisdiction, or of non-jurisdiction, or of high Prelacy. A Prelate, who possesses full ordinary jurisdiction, "does not, as a rule, wear this garment within the limits of his jurisdiction. [1]

The Pope never makes use of the mantelletta, because his jurisdiction is universal. Cardinals do not wear it outside of Rome; but they wear it in Rome on account of the Pope's presence. [2] However, in their own *titles,* where their jurisdiction is not limited, they do not I make use of the mantelletta. [3]

An Archbishop or a Bishop, outside of the territory of his jurisdiction, should not wear the rochet, unless it is covered with the mantelletta. [4] Therefore, all Titular Archbishops and Bishops, as well as Residential Bishops outside of their own dioceses, should not appear in their choir-habit without the mantelletta. [5] Even in his own diocese, a Bishop sometimes wears the mantelletta, namely, in the presence of a Cardinal, [6] in which case, he puts on the mantelletta under the mozzetta; but, if the Cardinal be a Legate *a latere*, the Bishop puts aside the mozzetta and keeps only the mantelletta over the rochet. [7] In no other case should the mantelletta be worn by an Archbishop or Bishop within the limits of his own jurisdiction. [8]

As a symbol of high Prelature, the mantelletta is worn by those Prelates who occupy the first rank at the Roman Court, and are, for that reason, known as *Prelates di mantelletta,* namely, the Protonotaries Apostolic of the three higher classes (*di numero, supernumerary* and *ad instar participantium*), the Votantes of the Signature, the Referees of the Signature, the Auditors of the Rota, the Clerks of the Reverend Chamber Apostolic, and all the other Domestic Prelates who do not belong to a "College." [9]

3. A Cardinal's mantellettas, like all the other parts of his choir dress, are of three different colors, scarlet, purple with red trimmings, and rose-colored, thus matching the colors of his cassocks. The red and purple mantellettas are of cloth in winter and of watered silk in summer. The rose-colored mantelletta, as well as the cassock of that color, is reserved for the Sundays of *Gaudete* and *Laetare,* and should be of watered silk.

Silk is not permitted as the material for the mantelletta of Bishops, [10] unless they be "Assistants at the Pontifical Throne." The ordinary episcopal mantelletta is of broadcloth or merino, according to the season, and purple or black, as may be called for by the Liturgy. The same rules hold good for the color of the mantelletta as for that of the choir cassock. The purple mantelletta is always trimmed and lined with crimson red silk; and the black mantelletta, with purple.

The Bishops Assistants at the Pontifical Throne, while living in Rome, and the Prelates *di mantelletta,* both in

Bishop wearing the Mantelletta over the Rochet

Rome and outside, wear the costume prescribed by the etiquette of the Papal Household, which includes a silk mantelletta in summer and one of fine broadcloth in winter, The color of this mantelletta is always purple, except during the vacancy of the Holy See and on Good Friday, when it is replaced by a black cloth mantelletta, trimmed and lined with purple silk. [11]

4. Cardinals and Bishops who belong to Religious Orders wear a mantelletta of a color like that of the outer part of the habit of the Order. [12] Abbots generally follow the same rule.

The Titular (or Honorary) Protonotaries Apost olic have the privilege of wearing the mantelletta; but their mantelletta is exclusively of black woolen material, lined and trimmed with black silk, purple being absolutely prohibited to them, as they are but diocesan Prelates. [13] Before the *motu proprio* of Pius X. (February 21, 1905), they had no right to make use of the rochet, and consequently they wore the mantelletta directly over the choir cassock; but, by that *motu proprio,* Pius X, conceded them the privilege of wearing the rochet under the black mantelletta. By the same act, the Pope entitled all the Vicars General and Vicars Capitular of dioceses, during the time they are in office, to the rank, costume and privileges of Honorary Protonotaries Apostolic ("Black Protonotaries"); the choir dress of these dignitaries consists, therefore, of a black choir cassock, the rochet, and the black mantelletta; unless they hold higher rank in the Prelature, in which case they wear the costume proper for the class of Prelates to which they belong. [14]

5. Some Chapters have obtained the special privilege of wearing the mantelletta; [15] but, in this case, the mantelletta is not a sign of Prelacy; it is only a part of their insignia as Canons. As such, it can not lawfully be worn outside of the diocese (except can. 409., § 2) nor should its use be extended beyond the express terms of the indult of concession.

[1] *Caer. Episc.* L.I.,1. I., IV.

[2] Un Évêque Suffragant, *op. cit.,* p. 4. - Barbier de Montault, *op. cit.,* Tom. I., p. 351. - Grimaldi, *op. cit.,* ch. VII., p. 112. - Other authors.

[3] The same references.

[4] *Caer. Episc.* I., I., 2, 3. - I., IV., 7. - All authors.

[5] S. R. C., Sept. 23, 1 842, *in Liburnen.*

[6] *Caer. Episc.* I., iv., 2, 3, 7.

[7] *Caer. Episc.* I., iv., 7. What is said here of a Bishop in his diocese also applies to an Archbishop within his province.

[8] S. R. C., Sept. 18, 1666, in *Orestan.*

[9] A. Battandier, *Annuaire Pontifical* (yearly). - "*Gerarchia*" (yearly). - Baart, *The Roman Court,* p. 277. Grimaldi, *op. cit.,* ch. V., pp. 58, seq.

[10] *Caer. Episc.* I., i., 1. I..III., 1.

[11] Barrier de Montault, *op. cit.,* Tom. I., p. 352, n. 4.

[12] *Caer. Episc.* I., i., 4.

[13] Const. *Inter multiplices* (Feb. 21, 1905), n. 64.

[14] Const. *Inter multiplices,* n. 62. In the United States, the Administrator of a vacant diocese, having the privileges of a Vicar Capitular, is therefore entitled to the rank, honors and costume of a "Titular Protonotary" during his tenure of office.

[15] The Chapter of the Cathedral of Rodez (France) and several Chapters in Italy have been granted that privilege.

Chapter Nine - Mantellone

1. The *mantellone* [1] is a kind of long purple mantle covering the cassock and reaching to the feet. It is open in front, and its collar, which fits around that of the cassock, is fastened with a hook. Two lateral openings permit the insertion of the arms, and two strips or bands, not more than four inches wide, of the same material as that of the mantle, hang on the back from the shoulders down to the heels. These strips simply recall the sleeves which were formerly attached to the vestment. It may be that the mantellone was frequently thrown over the shoulders, instead of being put on as a coat, and so, the sleeves became a sort of useless appendage. [2]

The mantellone is always of purple material, plain silk in summer, and light cloth in winter. Its lining and trimmings should never be red, but purple. Custom, however, permits that they be made of a different shade of purple. [3]

2. The mantellone is the proper garment of those dignitaries who hold a secondary rank at the Papal Court, and are called, on account of the costume they wear, "Prelates *di mantellone*."

Mantellone

The complete list of the different classes of these Prelates has been given in the first chapter of this book. It comprises the ecclesiastical chamberlains and chaplains of the Sovereign Pontiff, all of whom, with the exception of those styled *extra Urbem* (outside the City), are allowed to wear their prelatial costume both in Rome and outside. Those *extra Urbem* are never permitted to wear their prelatial insignia within the city limits of Rome, nor, strictly speaking, to be addressed, while there, as "Monsignor"; but they enjoy all those rights outside the city of Rome.

The Prelates *di mantellone* are not allowed the use of the rochet; they wear the mantellone directly over the purple cassock. This constitutes the etiquette costume of these Prelates when on duty at the Vatican, and their choir-habit elsewhere outside of the papal chapels. When performing ecclesiastical functions or administering sacraments, they lay aside the mantellone and wear a surplice or a *cotta* over the purple cassock, for the mantellone is a livery garment and should not be worn with liturgical vestments like the surplice or the rochet. Should a Prelate *di mantellone* have obtained the personal privilege of wearing the rochet, he should not wear it with the mantellone; but use it only for the celebration of Mass or the administration of the sacraments, in which latter case, he should wear the surplice (or *cotta*) over the rochet.

3. As was remarked before, the appointment of these Prelates lasts only during the lifetime of the reigning Pontiff; when he dies, they *ipso facto* lose their Prelacy, but they are readily reinstated by the new Pope, if application is made to that effect. Exceptionally however, some Prelates *di mantellone* are appointed for life; but this favor is entirely personal and does not militate against the general rule.

The title of the Prelates *di mantellone* is not that of *Illustrissimus et Reverendissimus* (Right Reverend), like that of the Domestic Prelates, but only that of *Illustrissimus et Reverendus,* corresponding to our English title "Very Reverend".

Whereas, according to strict etiquette, their stockings and hat cords should at all times be black; still an immemorial custom approved by Pope Clement VIII., allows them to wear purple stockings, and also purple cords around their hats, but outside of Rome only. The cloak (*ferraiolone*) is always black.

4. This chapter being devoted to the Prelates *di mantellone,* we must mention

Crocia Cf, a Prelate Di Mantellone.

here a peculiar garment worn by these Prelates on certain occasions the special *cappa,* otherwise called '*crocia*", which they wear in official ceremonies in the Vatican.

This *cappa* - or *crocia* - consists of a large outer dress, open in front, reaching to the feet, with wide, short, cuffed sleeves. The collar is fastened in front with a hook, and over the shoulders is placed a plain closed cape of ermine. This cape is of peculiar shape, different from that of a Bishop's or a Canon's *cappa magna*. It consists of two superposed capes, the lower of which is some inches longer than the upper. Formerly both capes were made of ermine, but as this fur is expensive and warm, the lower cape is now generally made of silk, with only that part covered with ermine, which is visible to the eye. The upper cape is entirely of ermine, and covers the hood, which is attached to the lower cape, permitting merely the top of the hood to be seen. During summer, these capes are replaced by others of the same shape, but entirely made of red silk.

This *cappa* is of scarlet woolen material, with lining, trimmings and cuffs of amaranth red silk. The *cappa* of *Consistorial Advocates,* which has nearly the same shape, is purple with red trimmings.

The *cappa* of the Prelates *di mantellone* is worn directly over the purple cassock. It is used only in the City of Rome, at the Papal Chapels, or consistories, and, outside of Rome, when the Prelate acts as the special delegate of the Sovereign Pontiff; for instance, when he is charged to deliver the red biretta to a newly-appointed Cardinal living outside of the Roman Curia.

5. We may end this chapter by remarking that the Prelates *di mantellone* are called "Prelates only by courtesy and have no part in the privileges granted to Prelates by Pope Pius X. in his Constitution *Inter multiplices,* the full text of which is given in the Appendix to this book. They must therefore wear an entirely black biretta, like all other priests, and abstain from making use of the hand-candlestick in church functions. Formerly, they were not even entitled to wear the purple *collaro;* but they now are granted that privilege, by the Sacred Congregation of the Ceremonial.

[1] An Italian word meaning *"a large mantle."*
[2] Grimaldi, *Congrégations romaines,* Chap. VII., p. 85, and note. - A. Battandier, *Annuaire Pontifical,* years 1899 and 1900.
[3] Grimaldi, *loc. cit.*

Chapter Ten - Cappa Magma

1. "Cappa magna" literally means a large cope or cape. The word "cappa" is a term of low latinity, said to be derived from *"capere"* (quia *capit* totum hominem - "because it covers the whole person"), and was originally used by ecclesiastical writers to denote the *pluviale* or *cope,* as appears from Durandus and Hononus. [1]

There is no English word translating "cappa." The only proper word would be "cope" and, as a matter of fact, "cope" was derived from "cappa;" but since this word is reserved, in ecclesiastical terminology, for the liturgical vestment, which the Rubrics call "*pluviale*," it is necessary to have recourse to the foreign term "cappa."

2. The cappa magna is a large mantle with a long train. It is entirely closed, with the exception of a vertical opening about ten inches long over the breast, and completed with a furred cape closed in front, slightly opened at the back, and fastened at the back of the neck with a hook. [2] To the cape a hood is attached, the use of which is determined by the Ceremonial of Bishops. [3] When not in use, this hood is caught up on the right shoulder and fastened there by a row of buttons and silk loops.

Formerly, the entire garment was lined with fur in order to protect the wearer from the cold; about the thirteenth century, hoods assumed a cape form by being allowed to fall back over the shoulders, whereby the fur lining became outermost, and it may be stated as a general principle that whatever fur appears on a Prelate's dress is supposed to be the winter lining. In summer therefore, when fur is not used, the portion of the Prelate's dress, which in winter is adorned with fur, must show, instead of the fur, the regular summer lining of silk.

Cappa Magna

Such is the case for the cappa magna. Although, for several centuries, the body of this garment has had no lining, still the fur is supposed to be the winter lining of the cape; therefore the fur cape must be substituted, in summer, by a similar cape of silk of the same material and color as the lining of the mozzetta or mantelletta which the Prelate wears on festival days. [4]

The outside of the cape, visible to the eye, being the lining (whether fur or silk), it follows that the other side, which is concealed, must be made of the same material and color as the body of the cappa magna.

Some tailors cut slits at the sides of the cappa magna to pass the arms; but this should not be done; the cappa magna is an entirely closed garment with no other opening than the vertical slit in front. When the Prelate stands or walks, he holds the fore part of the cappa lifted over his arms; when seated or kneeling, he lets it down and is thus entirely covered with the cappa (*capit totum hominem*); he may however pass his hands through the opening in front, if necessary. This, it must be admitted, is not very convenient if the Prelate wishes to read his breviary; but a Prelate presiding over a ceremony is not supposed to read his private office.

3. There are two styles of cappa magna, the one fully displayed, the other curtailed and folded.

The former - the one above described - is the cappa which we are accustomed to see worn by a Bishop in his diocese. This cappa is a sign of jurisdiction and authority; therefore, it is worn by the Pope and Cardinals everywhere; by a Metropolitan Archbishop, in his province; by a Bishop, in his diocese. [5] When the Prelate is sitting, the vestment is fully unfolded and gracefully draped around him, "covering the whole person." Whenever the Prelate walks, the train of the cappa must be carried by a train-bearer.

The train-bearer is supposed to be a cleric; he may be a seminarian, a member of the Prelate's household or even an altar boy, not a "page" in fancy costume, and there should be only one. The Pope having only one train-bearer, no other Prelate is entitled to have more. The dress of the train-bearer varies according to the different occasions on which he performs his duties. When accompanying a Cardinal to the papal" chapel, he vests in a purple cassock of silk, with trimmings and buttons of black velvet; he wears a purple silk cincture and a purple collaro; over the cassock, he puts, on the *crocia,* a surtout of peculiar shape, made of purple cloth or serge, lined and trimmed with purple silk. When the Pope officiates, the Cardinals vest in the sacred vestments of their orders - cope for Cardinal-Bishops, chasuble for Cardinal - Priests and dalmatic for Cardinal-Deacons; the train-bearers then put on a cotta over the crocia, and throw on their shoulders the *vimpa,* a long humeral veil of light silk with which they hold the Cardinals mitres. When a Cardinal officiates outside of the papal "chapels," his trainbearer does not wear the crocia, but the cotta over his purple cassock; and, when the Cardinal assists in cappa magna at a ceremony, the train-bearer wears over his purple cassock the ferraiolo of black silk. The train-bearer of the diocesan Bishop does not wear the crocia, which is a garment used only at papal "chapels;" but he wears the purple cassock with the black ferraiolo when the Bishop is vested in cappa magna, and the cotta over the purple cassock when the Bishop is dressed in his pontificals. In no case should he wear gloves or a biretta. [6]

The other cappa, curtailed and folded, is worn by Bishops and certain Prelates *di mantelletta* when attending the Papal "Chapels," and also by Canons, to whom it is conceded by a special indult of the Pope.

The cape of this cappa is similar to that of the other; but the vestment itself is so curtailed that it is reduced to a wide plaited band hanging on the back and ending in a short train. This train, however, is never let down, for the flowing train is a mark of jurisdiction; it is lifted up, twisted and tied with a purple ribbon, with which it is suspended from the left side of the cape. Thus twisted and tied up, this train symbolizes a restricted jurisdiction, or absence of jurisdiction. [7]

Formerly there was no difference between these two styles of *cappa;* this is why the regulations laid down for the use of the one apply also to the other.

4. The Pope's cappa magna is not white, as some may believe, but red. He wears it only when attending the Matins of Christmas, the Office of the Dead, and the *Tenebrae.* On Christmas night, his cappa magna is of red velvet, and of red serge for funeral services and *Tenebrae.* [8]

5. Cardinals wear a silk cappa magna during the entire year, except on Good Friday, when they should wear a cappa of woolen material. [9] A Cardinal's cappa magna, red at ordinary times, is purple during the

Prelate wearing the folded cappa

penitential season, on days of mourning, and when attending funeral services. [10] In Rome, Cardinals wear the red cappa magna in their *titles* and when attending the Papal "chapels," held in the Pontifical Palace. [11] Should the Papal chapel be held outside of the Pontifical Palace, etiquette would require that Cardinals wear the purple cappa magna; but for this, as for many other points of Roman ceremonial, the Cardinals who are to attend a solemn function receive detailed instructions beforehand from the pontifical Master of Ceremonies.

When at Rome, Cardinals have a special trainbearer belonging to the "Confraternity of Train-Bearers." [12]

6. The Ceremonial of Bishops contains full information on the use of the cappa magna by Bishops. The episcopal cappa magna is exclusively made of

woolen material and always purple, even in penitential season (*ut sint [cap-pae]... lameae et violaceae et non alterius coloris*). [13] No custom authorizes the wse of a silk cappa magna by a Bishop.

7. Cardinals and Bishops belonging to Religious Orders are not allowed the use of a red or purple cappa magna. Their cappae, made of woolen material, are of the same color as the outer part of the Order habit. The cape is sometimes of ermine, namely, when the lining of the prelatial dress is white; but, as a rule, it is made of other furs, matching the color of the cappa, as those of the vicunia, otter, northern cat, or Russian blue fox. For these furs, silk of the same color is substituted in summer. [14]

Abbots who have the privilege of wearing the cappa magna ought to follow the same rules, unless the papal concession includes special regulations.

Bishops belonging to Religious Congregations or to Orders of Clerics Regular may wear the same style of cappa magna as secular Prelates; [15] but the cappa magna of a Cardinal belonging to the same Congregations or Orders must not be made of silk, like that of a secular Cardinal, since that material is forbidden to the Religious; his cappa magna, while conforming to that of the secular Cardinals as to colors, must be made of woolen material like a Bishop's.

8. The Bishop must be vested in the cappa magna when he goes to the cathedral on feast days; and, where the cathedral is canonically constituted, having a Chapter, the Bishop vested in cappa magna has a strict right to be escorted by the Chapter as a body, and to have as assistants two Canons. [16] If he does not wear the cappa magna, he has no right to these honors. When vested with the mozzetta, he takes his seat in the first stall of the choir; [17] but, when he wears the cappa magna, he sits upon his throne. [18]

The hood of the cappa magna is used to protect the head from cold when the Prelate assists at Matins a rather rare occurrence in our days and, as a sign of mourning, when he goes to church, the last three days of Holy Week. [19] When giving his blessing from the throne, the Bishop covers his head with his biretta, or with the hood of the cappa, as a sign of authority. Another occasion, on which the hood of the cappa is used, is when the Prelate wears the pontifical hat, as this hat is not worn directly over the head, but over the hood of the cappa magna.

In Rome, at Papal "chapels" held in the Apostolic Palace, Cardinals wear the unfolded cappa magna; Archbishops, Bishops, the Prelates di fiochetti, Protonotaries Apostolic, the Votantes and Referees of the Signature, the Auditors of the Rota, the Clerks of the Reverend Chamber Apostolic and the Ministers of the papal chapel wear over the rochet the curtailed cappa magna. Visiting Archbishops and Bishops are however allowed to wear the mantelletta, for the reason that they usually lack the cappa required for the occasion. At such ceremonies, the Prelates *di mantellone* appear in the special red cappa - *cro-cia* - described in the preceding chapter. [20] As Cardinals are privileged to let down the train of the cappa magna in presence of the Pope, they have a train-bearer, whose duty it is not only to carry the train of the Cardinal's cappa, but also to hold his biretta, his breviary, papers, etc., when necessary. A Cardinal never wears his biretta in presence of the Pope, so the train-bearer holds it all the time at Papal chapels. Those who wear the folded cappa at Papal chapels never let down its train, except on Good Friday at the adoration of the Cross; and, when these Prelates perform some liturgical function at the chapel, they do not wear the cappa, but put on the cotta over the rochet; Bishops, who serve the Mass of the Pope, or receive holy communion from his hand on Holy Thursday, observe the same rule. [21]

9. Canons, who wear by privilege the cappa magna, are not entitled to wear the episcopal cappa. It is understood that the cappa conceded to Canons is the folded one; and they are never allowed to let down its train, except for the adoration of the Cross on Good Friday, as was mentioned for the Prelates attending Papal "chapels;" and, as regards the occasions on which to wear the cappa, they are expected to follow faithfully the terms of the indult. The cappa, with an ermine cape, is a winter garment, as was said; therefore, Canons should not wear it in summer, but should substitute the cotta for the cappa over the rochet, unless they have received the very explicit privilege of using a summer cappa, that is the same style of cappa with a cape of silk instead of fur, in which case they wear the cape of fur in winter and the cape of silk in summer. [22] Moreover, as the cappa is a choir ornament and not a liturgical garment, if a Canon has to perform ecclesiastical functions, or to administer some sacrament, he should leave aside his cappa and wear instead the cotta over the rochet. [23]

[1] Durandus Mimaten., *Rationale divinorum officiorum,* Book III., ch. I., n. 13. - Honorius Augustodunen., *Opera liturgica,* Book I., ch. 227 (in Migne, P. L., vol. 172, col. 612). - Catholic Dictionary, *art.* "Cappa Magna."

[2] Levavasseur-Haegy, *Fonctions Pontificales,* Tom. I., p. 439 (edition 1904).

[3] *Caer. Episc.* II., v., 1. - II., XXII., 3, etc.

[4] *Caer. Episc.* I., III., 3.

[5] Barbier de Montault, *op. cit.,* Tom. I., p. 361. - S. R. C., Novemb. 22, 1643.

[6] Caer. Episc., I., XV. 1. - S. R. C., Aug. 2, 1608. - Jan. 24, 1660. – March 13, 770. - Martinucci, *Manuale Sacrarum Caeremoniarum,* Book V., ch. IV., n. 10. - Grimaldi, *op. cit.,* ch. VIII., p. 115 (footnote).

[7] Barbier de Montault, *loc. cit.* - Fisquet, *op. cit.,* passim.

[8] Un Évêque Suffragant, *op. cit.,* pp. 345-346.

[9] Barbier de Montault, *op. cit.,* T. I., pp. 361-362.

[10] On the third Sunday of Advent (*Gaudete*) and on the fourth Sun day of Lent (*Laetare*), when Cardinals wear a church-dress of rose colored silk, they wear the purple cappa magna.

[11] A "chapel" is a religious ceremony performed or presided over by the Pope. When the Pope officiates, he has, as Assistant Priest, the senior Cardinal-Bishop; as Deacon, one of the Cardinal-Deacons; and, as Subdeacon, one of the Auditors of the Rota.

[12] The train-bearers of Cardinals in Rome belong to a confraternity which has a Cardinal -Protector, and the prefect of which is the Pope's train-bearer. They have charge of the church of San

Salvatore *in campo*. - Barbier de Montault, Traité de la Construction, Tom. II., p. 531. - Grimaldi, *op. cit.*, ch. VIII., p. 115 (text and foot-note).

[13] *Caer. Episc.* I., iii., 3.

[14] S. R. C., 1628. - Martinucci, *Man. Caer.*, Book V., chapt. II., pp. 9-12. - Barbier de Montault, *op. cit.*, Tome I., p. 266.

[15] *Caer. Episc.* I., iii., 4.

[16] S. R. C., Sept. 2, 1597. - Jan. 13, 1646 - Sept. 13, 1646 - Jan. 12 1647 - March. 22, 1862 - March 22, 1894. - *Caer. Episc.*, I., iv., 7.

[17] S. R. C, July 24, 1638. - November 6, 1906.

[18] *Caer. Episc.* II., ix., 4.

[19] *Caer. Episc.*, II., xxii., 3.

[20] H. Fisquet, *Cérémonies de Rome*, pp. 43, 138, 139, 198, 229, etc.

[21] Un Évêque Suffragant, *op. cit.*, p. 18.

[22] Many decrees of the Sacred Congregation of Rites have been issued on this point.

[23] S. R. C., November 29, 1856, and. many other decrees.

Chapter Eleven - Hats

1. There are two kinds of prelatial hats, one, which we may call the "usual hat", is worn in civil life and generally outside of church ceremonies; the other, known as the "pontifical hat", is one of the official tokens of a Prelate's dignity, and is, nowadays, very seldom used, if at all. There can be no doubt that some three or four centuries ago, there was no real difference between the "usual" and the "pontifical" hats; but the former underwent gradual changes by following the fluctuations of fashion, while the latter retained its early form and color; and since, at the present time, they differ so much in shape and use, they must be studied separately.

The Usual Hat

2. The "usual" clerical hat is familiar to all persons who have travelled in countries where clergymen wear the full ecclesiastical dress outside of their houses, such as Italy, France, Belgium and Spain. Although, according to local customs, it may slightly vary in some of its features, yet its shape and general appearance make it quite different from a layman's hat.

In the eighteenth century, it had assumed the triangular shape of the "cocked hat" familiar to us as worn by the heroes of the Revolution, and it generally retained this shape until the middle of the nineteenth century; but it has nowadays reverted to its earlier form of a round, broad-brimmed, low-crowned hat. In strict etiquette, it should be made of beaver hair; but, for reasons of general economy, and also for greater comfort in summer, it is frequently made of ordinary felt.

The usual hat is uniformly black for all ecclesiastics, except the Pope and Cardinals, as will be noted hereafter; but the crown is encircled with a silk band or cord, the color of which is indicative of the wearer's dignity. The cord seems now generally preferred to the band, it ends in two tassels which slightly hang in back a little to the left. That band or cord is red and gold for Cardinals; green and gold for Patriarchs and Archbishops; green for Bishops [1] and the Regent of the Apostolic Chancery; amaranth red for the first three classes of Protonotaries Apostolic [2]; purple for the Domestic Prelates [3] and, outside of Rome, for the Prelates *di mantellone;* black for Titular Protonotaries and all other ecclesiastics. We may add that, strictly speaking, the lining of the hat should be of the same color as the band or cord; but it is not always easy to make hatters comply with this last regulation.

3. The Pope, when riding or walking in his gardens, wears a red felt hat adorned with a gold band or cord ending in gold tassels; this hat is of the general form above described, but the brim is raised and held on both sides by small gold strings. [4]

The Pope's Hat

4. Cardinals, besides the usual black hat which they wear like all other Prelates, have another one of red felt to be used only when they wear the purple or red cassock; [5] but the reader must note that this red hat is different from the Cardinals' pontifical hat which is bestowed upon them as one of the principal insignia of their high dignity.

5. The clerical hat, as here described, rather than the biretta, is the proper head-dress for a Prelate wearing his official costume outside of church ceremonies; and, since the wearing of the full ecclesiastical dress on public occasions is now accepted by public opinion in this country, there is no reason why the hat should not be included; the biretta should be confined to private wear at home and to official use in church ceremonies attended by a Prelate in choir dress.

The Pontifical Hat

6. The "usual hat" must not be mistaken for the "pontifical hat"; the former is an ordinary head-covering, without any symbolical meaning, while the latter is a token of dignity or jurisdiction, to be worn only in official ceremonies. [6]

Since 1870, however, the use of the pontifical hat has become almost completely obsolete, for it was worn by Cardinals and Prelates at the solemn cavalcades held on the occasion of the Pope's inauguration and at other papal pageants, ceremonies which no longer take place since the Pope has been deprived of his temporal power. The discontinuance of the wearing of the pontifical hat in Rome has caused its gradual abolition elsewhere; but it was formerly used on the inauguration of Cardinals, on a Bishop's solemn entry into his episcopal city, and when the Bishop went solemnly to his cathedral on feast days. [7]

The picture of the pontifical hat which illustrates this article shows the hat in its normal shape and proportions; but, owing to the disuse into which the hat has now fallen, its crown has gradually become very small, measuring not more than four inches in diameter at the base, and two inches in height. The tasselled cords which hang on each side of the crown are meant to fasten the hat on the wearer's head, a necessary precaution indeed, when one remembers that the pontifical hat was worn principally when the Prelate rode on horseback in a solemn procession. The illustration shows the hat cords ending in simple tassels; but the tassels often are elongated and multiplied in triangular formation, after the style shown in the chapter on Heraldry; the tassels of a Cardinal's hat being most elaborate.

The Pope's pontifical hat is made of red velvet. [8]

The pontifical hat of a Cardinal is also red, but made of broadcloth. It is this hat which is properly the sign of the cardinalitial dignity. Cardinals were granted this red hat by Pope Innocent IV., at the first council of Lyons, A. D. 1245. [9] It is solemnly conferred by the Pope upon the newly-appointed Cardinals, at one of the consistories following their appointment. At the death of a Cardinal, his pontifical hat must be placed at the foot of the catafalque, and, afterwards, suspended from the ceiling above his tomb.

In Rome, Cardinals have another hat of a peculiar form, very large and with a small crown, made of red silk and bordered with gold. It is called in Italian "capellone" (a large hat). It is supposed to be used to protect the Cardinal from the sun when he walks bareheaded in processions, a valet holding it over the Cardinal's head. In fact, it is never used, except as a mark of dignity, on great occasions, as, for instance, the ceremonies of canonizations, when it is carried behind the Cardinal by the *decano* (dean) of his household, who holds it suspended from his left arm. [10]

The pontifical hats of Patriarchs, Archbishops and Bishops are made of green silk, with strings and tassels of the same color. The strings and tassels of the hats of Patriarchs and Archbishops are green, entwined with gold. [11]

Strict etiquette requires that the upper part of the hats of Patriarchs, Archbishops and Bishops should be made of black cloth, [12] and the under part, of green silk; but this prescription has hardly ever been observed, so that the pontifical hat of these Prelates is entirely green.

The Bishop's green hat is a sign of jurisdiction, and, consequently, not to be worn outside the limits of his diocese. [13]

On the Bishop's death, his pontifical hat is placed at the foot of the catafalque, and, after his burial, is suspended above his tomb. [14]

According to a decree of the Sacred Congregation of Rites, [15] the pontifical hat of the Protonotaries Apostolic of the first three classes is made of black cloth, with lining, borders, cords and tassels of amaranth red silk. [16] At the funeral of the Prelate, this hat is placed at the foot of the catafalque.

7. Besides the pontifical hat, the Protonotaries Apostolic of the first three classes have the privilege of wearing the "*Semipontifical*" or *Prelatial hat,* which differs from the preceding only in this, that it has a narrower brim. [17]

This hat is conceded also to the Votantes and Referees of the Signature, and to the Masters of Ceremonies of the Apostolic Palace. But while the semipontifical hat of the Protonotaries Apostolic is trimmed with amaranth red silk, that of the Votantes, Referees and Masters of Ceremonies is trimmed with purple.

Both pontifical and semi-pontifical hats are worn only when the Prelate is vested in the cappa magna; he puts the hood of the cappa on his head and the hat over it, then he ties the strings under his chin, the tassels hanging over his breast. But all these regulations have only an academic interest, since the wearing of these official hats has now fallen into disuse.

8. Heraldry however has retained them. The pontifical and semi-pontifical hats being tokens of dignity, are placed over the coats-of-arms of the Prelates, [18] as will be seen further on.

[1] *Caer. Episc.* I., I., 3.

[2] Constit. *Inter multiplices,* February 21, 1905, nn. 16, 17.

[3] *Const. cit.,* n. 79.

[4] Barbier de Montault, *op. cit.,* Tom. I., p. 238. - J. de Narfon, *Léon XIII. intime,* ch. IV., p. 182. - And other authors.

[5] Barbier de Montault, *op. cit.,* Tom. I., p. 456. - Grimaldi, *op. cit..* ch. VIII., p. 115.

[6] *Caer. Episc.* I., iii., 5.

[7] *Caer. Episc.* I., II., 1. H. Fisquet, Cérémonies de Rome, *passim.*

[8] H. Fisquet, Ceremonies de Rome, *passim.*

[9] Ferraris, *Bibliotheca canonica,* art. *Cardinales,* II.

[10] Fisquet, Cérémonies de Rome, p. 199.

[11] The "Regent of the Chancery," though not invested with the episcopal character, is privileged to wear a hat similar to that of a Bishop.

[12] *Caer. Episc.* I., i. 1. - I., III., 5.

[13] S. R. C. Sept. 23, 1848.

[14] *Caer. Episc.* II., xxxviii., 13. - Barbier de Montault, *op. cit.,* Tom. II., p. 351.

[15] S. R. C, Febr. 7, 1707. - Pius IX.'s Constit. *Apostolicae Sedis* (1872). Pius X.'s Const. *Inter multiplices* (Febr. 21, 1905, n. 16). Barbier de Montault, *op cit.,* Tom. II., p. 351

[16] This hat was conceded to the Protonotaries Apostolic by Pope Clement X., Aug. 6, 1674. - *Annalecta Iuris Pont.,* 3d. S., col. 699.

[17] S. R. C., April 16, 1644.

[18] Innocent X.'s bull *Militantis Ecclesiae* (1644). - Pius X.'s Constit *Inter multiplices* (1905), nn. 18, 68, etc.. etc.

Chapter Twelve - Biretta

1. The biretta (beretta, *biretum, birettum*) is an ecclesiastical cap, square in shape, having three 4 horns" or projections on top, with a tuft ("*pom-pon*") of silk (not a tassel) attached where the three horns meet in the middle. In wearing the biretta, the part which has no horn should be to the left.

The form here described is the Roman, and the one generally adopted in this country.

2. The biretta is made of thin cardboard, covered with some light material, the color and quality of which are settled by rule.

This material must always be woolen in birettas of priests and clerics of lower rank.

Cardinals and Bishops have the use of two birettas, one covered with silk for summer, the other covered with light cloth for winter.

All Prelates, either *di mantelletta* or *di mantellone,* wear throughout the year a biretta covered with silk. [1]

3. The color of the biretta varies according to the rank and dignity of the wearer.

Until the Pontificate of Leo XIII., the biretta of Cardinals was red, and that of all the other members of the clergy was uniformly black. [2]

4. However, as many Bishops, Prelates and Canons had presumed to wear the purple biretta under different pretexts, Leo XIII., desirous of establishing a well-marked difference between Prelates invested with the episcopal character and those who were simply priests, granted the exclusive privilege of wearing a purple biretta to all Patriarchs, Primates, Archbishops and Bishops, no others having the privilege. [3]

The letter *"Praeclaro divinae gratiae,"* granting that favor, was issued on February 3, 1888. According to the terms of that document, the biretta is one of ordinary form, entirely purple; and no mention being made of red pipings or cords along the seams, such ornaments should not be added. In Rome, where official samples are carefully kept by hatters and tailors, these cords are unknown, and the tuft is of purple silk. From answers given by the Sacred Congregation of Rites, we gather that, if such cords are added, they must be of the same color as the biretta. [4]

As will be said when speaking of the Doctors cap, the episcopal biretta should not be made with four horns, for, though a Bishop is a Doctor of Divinity, his purple biretta is not a sign of his theological attainments, but of his episcopal character. [5]

5. Cardinals wear a red biretta at all times, no matter what the season of the year or the liturgical occasion. The Cardinal's biretta differs from the others in that it usually has no tuft; at the point where the three horns meet there is only a small loop of silk string.

The biretta that Cardinals wear is not the one they received from the Pope, as a token of their dignity, immediately after their promotion to the Cardinalate. Through respect for its origin, they do not wear this biretta sent by the Pope, but place it on a credence-table in their ante-chamber, between two candlesticks. [6]

6. With regard to the biretta of those Prelates who are not invested with the episcopal character, new regulations have been issued by Pope Pius X. in his *motu proprio* of February 21 , 1905. Speaking of the Protonotaries Apostolic of the first three classes, he says: "...*gestare valent...nigrum biretum, flocculo ornatum coloris rubini;*" ("they may wear a black biretta ornamented with a red-colored tuft"). [7] As to the other Prelates, they have acquired by virtue of the same *motu proprio* the privilege of ornamenting their black birettas, with a purple tuft: "...*nec alio uti colore quam violaceo in bireti flocculo.*" [8] The text of the decree is as clear as it is restrictive; it allows no other ornament to the black biretta but the red or purple pompon; it is therefore illegal to decorate a prelatial biretta with red pipings along the seams. As for the Prelates *di mantellone,* since they are not included in the classes of Prelates mentioned in the decree, they have no part in the privileges therein granted hence they have no right to wear birettas ornamented with a purple pompon; their birettas must be entirely black, custom permitting only a purple lining.

7. The lining of the biretta, though apparently a trifling matter, is, however, regulated by etiquette. A Cardinal's biretta is lined with scarlet red; and that of a Bishop, with green. Crimson red lining is reserved for the Prelates *di mantelletta*. Custom allows the Prelates *di mantellone* to use a biretta lined with purple; but the biretta of priests and ecclesiastics of lower rank should have no other lining than black.

[1] A biretta of velvet is in opposition to these principles, as has been already remarked.

[2] *Caer. Episc.* 1. i., 4.

[3] Const. *Praeclaro divinae gratiae,* February 3, 1888.

[4] S. R. C., Sept. 6, 1895, *in S. Iac. de Chile.* (*Biretum formae ordinariae ac coloris violacei, cum flocculo et funiculis eiusdem coloris* - a biretta of the ordinary form, and of purple, with tuft and cords of the same color.] S. R. C., Novemb. 26, 1919.

[5] S. R. C., Dec. 7, 1884, in *Venusina.* - Sept. 6, 1895, *in S. Iac. de Chile.*

[6] Barbier de Montault, *op. cit.,* Tom. I., pp. 232-233. - Un Évêque Suffragant, *op. cit.,* p. 5. - Grimaldi, *op. cit.,* ch. VIII., p. 119.

[7] Constitution *Inter multiplices* (Febr. 21, 1905), nn. 16, 45.

[8] Constitution *Inter multiplices* (Febr. 21, 1905), n. 79.

Chapter Thirteen - Calotte or Skull-Cap

1. The skull-cap (called also *calotte* or *zucchetto*) is a small cap used by Catholic clergymen to cover the tonsure. It is called in Latin documents "*pileolus.*" [1]

Strictly speaking, it should not be of any other material than cloth in winter and silk in summer, for all ecclesiastics, even Regulars; but, in practice, the silk calotte is permitted throughout the year.

Every ecclesiastic may wear a calotte; it is not reserved solely for Prelates. However, a calotte of another color than black is not permitted to priests and ecclesiastics of lower rank, as it is one of the insignia of the Prelacy.

2. The red skull-cap is one of the proper insignia of the Cardinalate, together with the red hat and the red biretta. And it is so exclusively reserved for Cardinals that the Pope, when granting, by special favor, to a Bishop the privilege of wearing a Cardinal's robes without making him a Cardinal, always excepts the use of the red skull-cap. More over, Cardinals taken from Religious Orders, what ever be the color of their cassocks, are entitled to wear the scarlet zucchetto, as well as the red hat and the red biretta, these being the proper marks of their dignity.

3. By the Brief *Ecclesiarum omnium* (June 17, 1867,) Pope Pius IX. granted to all Patriarchs, Archbishops and Bishops, the privilege of wearing the purple calotte, as an exclusive sign of the episcopal dignity, [2] and this privilege has been extended by canon 325 of the new Code of Canon Law to Abbots or Prelates *nullius*.

Skull-Cap

Soon after the Brief of Pius IX. was published, tailors and hatters, in making calottes, went beyond the concession, and began to add extra ornaments that are not mentioned in the Pontifical document. According to the official sample fixed at the time of the concession, the episcopal calotte should be entirely purple, without any addition of red cords or of red stitchings; there should be no cords, while the stitchings should be purple. The lining is of red leather.

4. Before the appearance of Pope Pius X.'s *motu proprio "Inter multiplices,"* all Prelates not invested with the episcopal character, or at least Bishops-elect, were allowed to wear only a black skull-cap; but Roman etiquette permitted that the lining be red for the calotte of the Prelates *di mantelletta,* and purple for that of the Prelates *di mantellone.* Pius X., by the above-mentioned *motu proprio,* granted to the Protonotaries Apostolic *di numero, supernumerary* and *ad instar,* a special skull cap, black, with cords of amaranth red silk along the seams, and stitchings of the same color. By the

same act, the other Prelates were conceded a like calotte, but with the said trimmings in purple.

5. The use of the calotte having been introduced for no other purpose than to cover the tonsure, in order to protect the head from cold, it follows that those who are not clerics are not entitled to wear this cap. For this reason, the custom of allowing sanctuary boys to wear the calotte has been frequently condemned by the Sacred Congregation of Rites.

6. The use of the calotte by Bishops is determined by the following rules: A Bishop is privileged to wear his skull-cap not only at home, but also in church, even when assisting at services and celebrating Mass. He always wears it under the mitre, in order to prevent the hair from soiling the inside of the mitre. [3]

When assisting at Mass in cope, he wears the calotte all the time, except during the consecration and elevation; [4] but, when assisting at Mass in choir habit (*cappa magna, mozzetta* or *mantelletta*), he removes his skull-cap, also at the reading of the Gospel and when he is incensed. [5]

Bishops are privileged to wear the skull-cap while celebrating Mass, except from the *Sanctus* until after communion. In this case the Bishop's skull-cap is taken off his head (at Low Mass by one of his servers, at High Mass by one of the officers) after he has recited the *Sanctus,* and replaced after he has taken the ablutions.

On all other occasions, the Prelate himself should remove and put on his calotte.

The wearing of the skull-cap is never allowed in presence of the Blessed Sacrament exposed; and Prelates are directed to remove the skull-cap every time they perform some external act of private devotion, as, for instance, genuflecting, kissing the crucifix or the relics of a saint. [6]

The Pope's Camauro

The same regulations hold good for Cardinals; but Cardinals alone have the privilege of wearing the skull-cap in presence of the Sovereign Pontiff; all other Prelates remain bareheaded in his presence in sign of obedience and respect, and even Cardinals, while bowing to him, remove their skull-caps.

7. The Pope makes use of a white skull-cap, similar in shape to that of other Prelates; but he has besides the exclusive privilege of wearing a cap special to him, called in Italian "camauro." The material for this cap is red velvet, with a border of ermine. During the octave of Easter, the red camauro is replaced by one of white damask. This cap has probably retained the primitive shape of the biretta. This would explain why the Pope does not make use of a biretta like other members of the Prelacy and clergy. [7]

[1] Latin documents and rubrics usually call it *pileolus,* but sometimes also *biretum,* and, in this case, the reader must carefully ascertain from the context whether the word *biretum* means the skull-cap or the biretta described in the preceding chapter.

[2] Leo XIII, made an exception to this rule when he conceded the use of the purple calotte to the Abbot of Solesmes and his successors for ever. From time to time, the Pope grants the same privilege to an Abbot as a mark of personal esteem; but the grant is not to be understood as extending to the successors of the Abbot thus distinguished.

[3] *Caerem. Episc., passim.*

[4] S. R. C., June 14, 1845 - Decemb. 5, 1848.

[5] S. R. C., May 20, 1890.

[6] A Bishop should not wear the skull-cap while imparting the blessing with a relic of the True Cross.

[7] Cfr. the interesting study of Mgr. A. Battandier in the "Annuaire Pontifical" for 1901, pages 76-81.

Chapter Fourteen - Stockings

1. There are two kinds of prelatical stockings, the *ordinary stockings,* worn by Prelates in daily life and church functions, and the *liturgical stockings* or *buskins,* worn by Bishops, and other Prelates having the privilege of the *pontificals,* [1] when they celebrate Pontifical Mass.

2. The ordinary stockings are knit of black, purple, red, or white silk, each Prelate wearing stockings that match the color of his choir cassock. Therefore, the Pope's stockings are white; the Cardinals, red; Bishops and Prelates *di mantelletta's,* purple; other members of the clergy wear black. Prelates belonging to Religious Orders wear stockings of the same color as their cassocks. [2]

Formerly, the color was changed, like that of the cassock, according to the liturgical season; but the present etiquette prescribes the wearing of the same color in stockings throughout the year. [3]

These stockings should regularly cover the feet and legs up to the knees, as they are supposed to be worn with "knickerbockers", and they are held by a garter above or below the knee; but, as they are inconvenient to wear with our long trousers, they may be substituted, in this country, by socks of the same material and color.

3. Purple or red stockings are, among the clergy, a mark of Prelacy. Therefore, no secular ecclesiastic who is not a Prelate has any right to wear other

stockings or socks than black; unless he has obtained a personal privilege, as is the case for certain Chapters in Europe. [4]

4. Though altar boys are vested in red or purple cassocks, they are not entitled to wear stockings of these colors under the pretext of matching the different parts of their church dress. If special stockings are given them for their functions in church, these stockings should be black. The same rule applies to all who wear a purple cassock as a livery-dress, including the Prelates *di mantellone*. [5]

5. Liturgical stockings, or *buskins,* are prescribed by the Rubrics and the Ceremonial of Bishops for the celebration of Pontifical Mass. [6] They differ from ordinary stockings, because they have preserved the antique form of stockings previous to the invention of knitting.

They are made of silk material, not knitted, but woven and tailored, and their color is the one required by the office of the day, white, red, green, or purple. [7] Such stockings are not used at Requiem Mass. [8]

All who, by virtue of their Orders, or by special privilege, are entitled to celebrate Pontifical Mass, wear these stockings. Those of the Pope and Cardinals may be embroidered with gold. Those of Archbishops, Bishops, Protonotaries Apostolic *di numero* and *supernumerary,* are made of plain silk and bordered with a gold strip. [9] Those of the Protonotaries *ad instar,* of Abbots, Canons, etc, may be trimmed with a strip of yellow silk only. [10]

Pontifical Buskin

The Prelate, while vesting for Pontifical Mass, puts on these buskins over his ordinary stockings or socks, and has them fastened to his leg with a silk ribbon sliding through loops at the top of the buskin; and, when the Prelate wears long trousers, as is the custom in this country, the lower part of the trousers should be folded so as to fit inside the legs of the buskin, thus avoiding the unsightly appearance of the pontifical sandals partly covered by the black trousers.

5. Cardinals, Prelates invested with the episcopal character, Abbots and the seven Protonotaries Apostolic *di numero,* put on the liturgical stockings at the throne or at the faldstool while reciting the prayer "*Calcea, Domine, pedes meos...*" [11]

Other Protonotaries, Canons and all ecclesiastics who may have received the privilege of celebrating Pontifical Mass, are not permitted to put on their liturgical stockings at the faldstool, but only in the sacristy. [12]

[1] The "pontificals" are marks of dignity that Cardinals and Bishops use when officiating at solemn High Mass. These are the stockings, sandals, ring, gloves, pectoral cross, mitre, crosier, tunics, hand-candlestick and gremial.

[2] The members of discalced Orders, like the Franciscans, Carmelites, Trinitarians, Passionists, etc., when promoted to the episcopate or cardinalate, must no longer go barefooted, but wear stockings and shoes like the other Prelates, even if they continue by choice to wear the habit of the Order.

[3] Barbier de Montault, *op. cit.*, Tom. I., pp. 61, 62. - On Good Friday, Cardinals are directed to wear purple stockings, and all other Prelates, black. - Battandier, *Annuaire Pontifical* (1903), p. 361.

[4] S. R. C., April 11, 1840. - S. C., Bish. and Reg., 1848. - Brief of Gregory XVI., June 8, 1841, etc.

[5] Clement VIII. granted to the Prelates *di mantellone* the privilege of wearing purple stockings outside of Rome.

[6] *Caer. Episc.* I., x., 2. II., viii., 7. - Rubric of the Missal.

[7] Pius VII.'s Const. *Decet Rom. Pont.* (1823).

[8] *Caer. Episc.* II., xi., 2.

[9] Barrier de Montault, *op cit.,* Tom. II., p. 263. - Pius X. Const. *Inter multiplices* (1905), n. 27.

[10] Pius X.'s *Const. cit.*, n. 47.

[11] Rubric of the Missal.

[12] Pius VII.'s Const. *Decet. Rom. Pont.* (1823).

Chapter Fifteen - Shoes

1. This chapter deals with two different sorts of prelatial footwear, the *shoes* worn by Prelates either in civil life or in church functions, and the *sandals* prescribed by the rubrics for the celebration of Pontifical Mass.

The ecclesiastical *shoe* is well known, for it has preserved the general appearance of the footwear in vogue at the beginning of the nineteenth century and still used as part of the court dress a low patent leather shoe, or "pump", with a large buckle in front.

Of course, this style of shoes cannot be worn with our modern American civilian dress, but it is quite proper to wear them on occasions when a Prelate or other clergyman appears in full ecclesiastical dress. [1]

Shoes of this kind, according to Roman etiquette, should be worn by all members of the clergy, and by those who have to discharge any ecclesiastical functions in church, as chanters, sacristans, etc.

The buckles of the shoes, for the inferior members of the clergy and the officers of the church, are made of polished steel; and for priests, monks, and Prelates belonging to Religious Orders, of silver. Gold or gilded silver buckles are reserved for secular Prelates.

2. A Cardinal's ordinary shoes are black, with a red border and red heels. When a Cardinal vests in his red cassock and cappa magna, he may wear shoes made entirely of red leather. Etiquette prescribes it at Rome on solemn occasions, for instance, when Cardinals attend solemn Pontifical chapels or consistories. [2]

Pontifical Sandal

3. It is well known that the Pope wears for every day shoes, red, thin-soled, flat-heeled slippers, made of cloth or silk, according to the season. On the vamp of these shoes a gold cross is embroidered, which faithful Catholics, admitted to a private audience, kiss after having made three genuflections, according to etiquette.

4. A few principles must here be laid down concerning pontifical sandals (*sandalia, compagi*). These are the footwear used at Pontifical Mass by Bishops and all who have, by law or special concession, the privilege of using the "pontificals." [3]

The shape of these sandals is that of low shoes, with a thin sole and a flat heel. They would be even more correct, and more in conformity with etiquette and tradition, if they had no heel at all. They are fastened with silk ribbons or strings, to the end of which are attached small gold tassels if the Prelate is a Cardinal, a Bishop, or a Protonotary Apostolic *di numero* or *supernumerary;* tufts or tassels of silk, if he is of a lower rank.

The Rubric prescribes that the color of the sandals should match that of the vestments, that is the color required by the office of the day; but at Requiem Masses the officiating Prelate does not wear the sandals.

These sandals should be made of silk; no Prelate is allowed sandals of velvet or of gold cloth, and the Pope and Cardinals alone have a right to wear sandals embroidered with gold or silver. Bishops and the Protonotanes Apostolic *di numero* and *supernumerary* may wear sandals bordered with a gold or silver strip; [4] but other Prelates who may have the privilege of the pontificals should wear sandals with no other ornament than a border of yellow silk braid.

5. We sometimes see Cardinals and Bishops wearing sandals with a gold cross embroidered on the upper; and even some handbooks dealing with liturgical matters seem to give this practice as legitimate; but it is a usurpation or a mistake against which all serious authors protest; the cross embroidered on the sandals being a special and personal privilege of the Sovereign Pontiff. [5]

6. The pontifical sandals, as well as the liturgical stockings, are to be used only at High Mass pontifically celebrated; [6] they go together and are prescribed by the same rubric. A Prelate is no more permitted to waive this rubric under the pretext of simplicity, than to celebrate Mass without the proper vestments.

7. The privilege of putting on the stockings and sandals at the throne or at the faldstool belongs to the Pope, Cardinals, Bishops, Abbots and the seven Protonotaries Apostolic *di numero*. The other Protonotaries, Prelates, Canons, etc., who may have been granted the privilege of the "pontificals," must put on their sandals in the sacristy. [7]

There is only one prayer to be said by the Prelate while putting on his stockings and sandals, the prayer a *"Calcea, Domine, pedes meos..."* It is not required to repeat it twice. [8]

[1] Such usage cannot with justice be regarded as savoring of vanity, for there is no more vanity in wearing the proper style of shoes than in putting on a purple cassock or a richly embroidered mitre; the proper rule for all to follow in this matter is to dress on all occasions according to church ordinances.

[2] Barbier de Montault, *op. cit.*, Tom. I., p. 70. - Martinucci, *op. cit.*, Book V.,p. 505.

[3] *Caer. Episc.* II., VIII., 7. - Rubric of the Missal. - Pontifical de *ordin. conf.*

[4] Pius X., Const. *Inter multiplices* (1905), n. 27.

[5] All authors *in loco*. - Cfr., especially Martinucci, *op. cit.*, Book VI., Appendix, p. 548, note (b).

[6] For the conferring of Sacred Orders, the rubrics direct the Bishop to vest in his pontificals, even if the Mass is celebrated *sine cantu*.

[7] Pius VII., Const. *Decet Rom. Pont.* (1823). Pius X., Const. *Inter multiplices* (1905), n. 27, 47.

[8] *Caer. Episc.* II., VIII., 7. Rubric of the Missal.

Chapter Sixteen - Gloves

1. This chapter does not deal with the gloves worn by Prelates or other clergymen in daily life. In this country, custom prevails for ecclesiastics to wear gloves of the same style and in the same circumstances as well-bred conservative laymen.

The gloves which come under church regulations are of two sorts, the gloves used by clergymen when wearing the full ecclesiastical dress, and the gloves which certain Prelates are directed by the rubrics to put on for the celebration of Pontifical Mass. The latter being known to liturgists as *pontifical gloves,* we may here designate the former by the name of *official gloves.*

2. The official gloves complete the costume of a Prelate, but they are not meant for church use; the Prelate wears them on public occasions outside of liturgical ceremonies, such as receptions, official visits, academic solemnities, and the like.

There are certain occasions however when a Prelate, while dressed in full costume, should not wear gloves. Court ceremonial forbids the wearing of gloves in presence of the Sovereign Pontiff or at the audience of a nation's ruler, and, since the Chief Executive of a Republic enjoys by law or common consent the honors given to the head of the State in a monarchy, it would be a breach of etiquette for an American Prelate to wear gloves when officially received by the President of the United States.

If the Prelate's rank in the sacred hierarchy entitles him to wear a ring, he must put it on over the glove, as the Bishop does at Pontifical Mass, so as not to deprive the priests and people of the opportunity of kissing the ring.

The official gloves do not differ in shape from those worn in civil life; but they are made of silk of the same color as that of the stockings which the Prelate is privileged to wear, that is, white for the Pope, red for Cardinals, purple for Patriarchs, Archbishops, Bishops and all Domestic Prelates, purple also for the Prelates *di mantellone* outside of Rome, and black for all other secular ecclesiastics. Cardinals and Bishops belonging to Religious Orders follow the same general rule and wear gloves matching the color of their stockings.

3. The *pontifical gloves,* called by the rubrics *chirothecae,* are legally worn by all Prelates who are entitled by their orders or by special privilege to celebrate Pontifical Mass. They are not necessarily different in shape from the official gloves, although they usually have a cuff which covers the lower part of the alb sleeve and gives them the appearance of gauntlets. [1]

These gloves are used at no service but the Pontifical Mass, and they must match in color the Mass vestments white, red, green or purple; there are no black gloves, for the pontifical gloves are not allowed at Requiem Masses.

The pontifical gloves are made of silk, and variously ornamented according to the solemnity of the occasion and the wearer's rank and dignity. For Cardinals, Prelates invested with the episcopal character and Abbots, the back of the glove is embroidered with a more or less elaborate cross or monogram; and the Protonotaries Apostolic of the first two classes (*di numero* and *supernumerary*) may wear pontifical gloves of silk bordered with a strip of gold braid; [2] but for all other Protonotaries, Prelates and Canons, who may be allowed, by law or privilege, the use of the pontificals, the gloves must be of plain silk without any special ornament. [3]

[1] Mgr. X. Barbier de Montault, *Les gants pontificaux.*, Tours, 1877.
[2] Const. *Inter multiplices,* n. 27.
[3] Const. *Inter multiplices,* n. 47.

Part III - Some Other Articles Pertaining to the Prelatial Dignity

Chapter One - Pectoral Cross

1. The *pectoral cross* derives its name from pectus (breast), because it is worn hanging over the breast. It is a mistake to call it "pastoral cross," as is sometimes done. This expression is incorrect, because the pectoral cross is not a sign of jurisdiction, as might be implied by the term "pastoral," but a sign of order or dignity. [1]

2. There are two different sorts of pectoral crosses, the *ordinary cross* and the *pontifical cross,* the former being worn in ordinary daily life, the latter in the ceremonies of the Church, and especially in the celebration of Pontifical Mass. Very often, this distinction is not strictly observed in practice, Bishops using the same cross both in their daily life and in church.

3. It is now the universal practice to wear the ordinary pectoral cross suspended at the neck with a gold chain. It should be simple, without precious stones, and it is not necessary that it contain relics of martyrs. It must be of Latin form, that is the upper part and the arms of equal length, and the lower part longer. An exception is made in favor of the Archbishop of Armagh, Primate of All Ireland," and the Patriarch of Lisbon; both are entitled, in virtue of an immemorial custom, to wear a pectoral cross with a double traverse. Some other Prelates wear a similar cross, but their right to do so is not officially recognized. [2]

The ordinary pectoral cross may be worn over the civilian dress and over the cassock and simar; it is also tolerated over the mantelletta and mozzetta; but, in spite of a very general practice, no pectoral cross is permitted to be worn over the cappa magna. [3]

Ordinary Pectoral Cross

All Prelates invested with the episcopal character are free to wear the ordinary pectoral cross; [4] also Abbots, in virtue of an immemorial custom; [5]

and, by a special grant of Pope Pius X., Cardinals who have not received the episcopal consecration. [6]

4. While the ordinary cross may be worn by Bishops and some Prelates in daily life; the *pontifical cross* is reserved for church ceremonies and especially for the celebration of Pontifical Mass, and as such, is permitted not only to Bishops, but to all who have received the privilege of officiating in the *pontificals*.

This includes, besides Bishops, Cardinals, Protonotaries Apostolic, Abbots and a great number of Canons.

The pontifical cross is suspended from a rather heavy cord, which may be fitted around the neck with a slide, and from the end of which hangs a tassel over the back. This cord is of gold for the Pope, Cardinals and Patriarchs; of green silk, entwined with gold

A Prelate wearing the Pectoral Cross suspended from a cord

[7] for Archbishops, Bishops, Prelates *nullius* and Abbots General; of red silk, entwined with gold, for Protonotanes Apostolic *di numero;* [8] of plain red silk for Protonotanes Apostolic *supernumerary;* [9] and of purple silk for Protonotaries Apostolic *ad instar.* [10] For Canons, the color is determined in each case by the indult of concession; generally it is black, entwined with gold. For the pontifical cross of simple Abbots, the color of the cord is determined by the traditions of the Order.

The pontifical cross is of Latin form; it must be hollow, for the prayer recited by the Prelate, when he puts it on, supposes that it contains relics of Saints, "...*hanc crucem sanctorum tuorum reliquiis refertam.*" [11] Through respect for these relics, and on account of the solemn occasions on which this cross is used, it is made of gold. That of the Pope, Cardinals, Bishops and Prelates *nullius,* may be studded with diamonds and other precious stones; that of Abbots and Protonotanes Apostolic *di numero* should be adorned with one

Pontifical Pectoral cross

gem only (*cum unica gemma*). [12] Other Prelates and Canons, who are privileged to pontificate, wear a cross of plain gold. [13]

5. The Ceremonial of Bishops and the Rubrics of the Missal prescribe that the Prelate put on the Pontifical cross over the alb, after having put on the cincture, and before taking the stole. It is precisely on account of the pectoral cross that the Prelate does not cross the stole over his breast. If he had to say Mass and had not at hand his pectoral cross, he should wear the stole, as simple priests do.

The Sacred Congregation of Rites several times forbade the wearing of the pectoral cross, and even of the very tassel of the cordon over the chasuble.

Protonotaries Apostolic, when they come to church for the sake of celebrating Pontifical Mass, may wear the pectoral cross over the *mantelletta*. [14]

6. The privilege of wearing the pectoral cross has been granted to a certain number of Chapters, both in Italy and elsewhere. Moreover, when a Chapter is favored with the concession of the *pontificals,* the *indult* always determines the time, circumstances and right of using them, and the Ordinary has the duty to prevent the express terms of the *indult* from being exceeded.

[1] We read in certain old ceremonials that a Bishop, outside the limits of his jurisdiction, should conceal his pectoral cross. This is a mistake. The pectoral cross is essentially a sign of order, not of jurisdiction. At the Vatican council, Pope Pius IX. ordered the Bishops to wear ostensibly their pectoral crosses even in his presence. *"Fuori le croci!"* he said, when noticing that some Bishops concealed their pectoral crosses, as he entered the hall where they were assembled.

[2] *Annalecta iuris pontificii,* 1896, col. 344.

[3] Barbier de Montault, *op. cit.,* Tom. I., p. 408. - S. R. C., August 17., 1916.

[4] Martinucci, *Man. Caer.,* Book V., ch. IV., n. 10.

[5] Ferraris, *Bibliotheca canonica,* art. Abbas.

[6] *Motu proprio* of Pius X. (May 25, 1905). - A. Battandier, *Annuaire Pontifical,* 1906, p. 156.

[7] Martinucci, *Man. Caer.,* Book V., ch. I., p. 6.

[8] Const. *Inter multiplices* (1 905), n. 8.

[9] *Const.* cit., n. 27.

[10] *Const.* cit., n. 47.

[11] Rubric of the Missal.

[12] *Const. cit.,* n. 8. - Some ceremonials teach that Cistercian Abbots should use pectoral crosses of wood; but this is against the universal practice of the Church and the real traditions of the Order.

[13] *Const. cit.,* n. 27 and 47.

[14] Const. *"Inter multiplices"* (Feb. 21, 1905), n. 7, 26, 46, 47.

Chapter Two - Ring

1. The ring, symbolizing the spiritual marriage of a Bishop and his church, has always been considered one of the principal insignia of the episcopal rank. [1]

However, the privilege of the ring has been granted to other dignitaries not invested with the episcopal character, namely, Cardinals, Abbots, [2] Prelates, [3] Canons [4] and Doctors. [5]

By all these dignitaries, the ring must be worn on the fourth finger of the right hand.

2. Let us first distinguish three classes of ecclesiastical rings, viz.: *pontifical, gemmed* rings, and *simple* rings.

The *pontifical ring*, denoted as *Annulus cordis* by the Rubric of the Missal, is the one used for the celebration of Pontifical Mass. It should be large enough to be put on easily over the gloved finger, [6] and ornamented with a beautiful large stone.

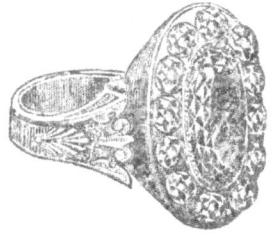

Pontifical Ring

The *gemmed* (or *ordinary*) ring is the one habitually worn by Bishops and Prelates. It is adorned with a simple gem, or with a large stone surrounded by brilliants, according to the rank of the dignitary.

The *simple ring* is one without gem, having a plain gold bezel, on which a coat-of-arms or initials may be carved, that it may be used as a seal. Such is the Doctors ring given by the Roman Universities. [7]

The Pope's ordinary ring adorned with a cameo.

(L) **The Ring of the Fisherman**
(Center) **Impression of the Fisherman's Ring** (actual size).
(R) **A Cardinal's Ring.** (Note the coat-of-arms of the Pope engraved inside.)

The *Ceremonial of Bishops* and the *Pontifical* suppose that Prelates wear several rings: "*Extractisque...annulis, lavat manus.*" [8] "*Depositis annulis et chirothecis, lavat manus, reassumit annulos...*" [9] And though the present discipline is in favor of only one ring, there is no written law opposed to the quoted passages of the *Ceremonial* and *Pontifical*.

3. The Pope makes use of the pontifical ring when he officiates at High Mass. His ordinary ring is adorned with a cameo or carved gem, which is the Pope's exclusive privilege. [10]

Another ring, peculiar to the Pope, is the Fisherman's ring, with which the Briefs are sealed. This ring has a large bezel on which is engraved a figure of St. Peter fishing, with the name of the reigning Pope in this form, Pius XI. Pont. Max. This ring is put on the Pope's finger as soon as he accepts his election to the Papacy; then, he immediately takes it off and gives it to the Master of Ceremonies, to have his new name en graved on it. *The Master of Chamber* is entitled to keep this ring, which is the Pope's private seal. But the *Secretariate of State* has a duplicate of it, so that the ring kept by the Master of Chamber is seldom used. [11]

On the Pope's death, the Fisherman's ring is solemnly broken. [12]

4. The Cardinals, besides the pontifical and ordinary rings, have a peculiar one, which they receive from the Pope when promoted to the Cardinalate. This ring is adorned with a sapphire (a stone reserved for Cardinals) and has the arms of the Pope engraved inside.

This ring is furnished by the *Propaganda,* to which the newly-promoted Cardinal must pay 600 *scudi* (about 3,000 lire, or $600), whereby he acquires the right of making his will. Otherwise, his property is inherited by the *Reverend Chamber Apostolic.* [13]

When a Prelate, having already the right to wear a ring, is created a Cardinal, Roman etiquette prescribes that he take off his ring and abstain from wearing it till he receives from the Pope a Cardinal's ring. [14]

5. Bishops, in virtue of their consecration, wear the pontifical ring when they officiate vested in their pontificals. In ordinary life, they wear a ring adorned with a large stone surrounded by brilliants. This stone may be of any kind, except sapphire, which is reserved for Cardinals.

A Bishop's ordinary ring.

6. Abbots have the same rings as Bishops, except that the ordinary ring has but a single gem. [15]

7. The seven Protonotaries Apostolic di numero are entitled to wear the ordinary ring with one stone, "*cum unica gemma,*" [16] and they wear also the pontifical ring when they officiate in their pontificals. [17] The Protonotaries Apostolic *supernumerary* and *ad instar* use the pontifical ring when they celebrate Pontifical Mass; but, outside of that function, they are not habitually allowed to wear a ring. [18]

8. Canons must follow the rules laid down by the indult granting them the favor of wearing the ordinary or pontifical ring.

9. According to Roman usage, Doctors have the right to wear a ring. Ordinarily the ring delivered by the Roman Universities is of plain gold, with the word ROMA engraved on the bezel. But this is only a local custom; no written law, custom or ceremonial prohibits Doctors from wearing a more elaborate ring, adorned with one or several gems. [19]

The use of a Doctor's ring is however strictly reserved for civil life, teaching, and academic solemnities. The Sacred Congregation of Rites has frequently forbidden the use of the doctoral ring during ecclesiastical ceremonies, even in the celeb ration of Low Mass. [20]

10. With regard to kissing a Bishop's hand, it is to be noted that it is the ring, and not merely the hand, of the Bishop, which is kissed, his ring being the symbol of his close union with his church, [21] as well as the sign of his authority, and, by decree of Pope Pius X. (March 18., 1909), an indulgence of 50 days, applicable to the souls in Purgatory, may be gained by devoutly kissing the ring of a Cardinal, Archbishop, or Bishop.

Should one bend the knee when kissing the episcopal ring? Yes, if the Bishop is within the limits of his own diocese, as it is an acknowledgment of his jurisdiction as *Ordinary*. Outside of his own diocese, etiquette requires that he should only permit a low bow due to his character as a Bishop

According to principles frequently laid down in this manual, it is proper to bend the knee to a Cardinal everywhere, to an Archbishop in his province, and to an Abbot in his monastery; and the same honor should also be paid to the Apostolic Delegate throughout the territory of his Delegation.

---

[1] Pontif. Rom., de *Consecratione electi in Episcopum.*

[2] Several bulls of Pope Urban II. (eleventh century).

[3] S. R. C., March 3, 1674, etc. - *Const. Decet Rom. Pont.* - Const. *Apostolicae Sedis.* - Const. *Inter multiplices,* etc., etc.

[4] In Italy, almost all Canons wear a ring.

[5] S. R. C., May 23, 1846, etc. - A. Battandier, *Annuaire Pontifical* (1906), pp. 449, seq.

[6] *Caer. Episc.* II., viii., 11.

[7] Barbier de Montault, *op. cit.,* Tom. I., p. 159. - A. Battandier, *Annuaire Pontifical* (1906), p. 449.

[8] *Caer. Episc.* II., VIII., 10.

[9] Roman Pontifical, de *ord. confer.*

[10] Barbier de Montault, *op. cit.,* Tom. I., p. 161, n. 6.

[11] Barbier de Montault, *loc. cit.* - Grimaldi, *op. cit.,* ch. IV., p. 49; ch. XXVII., p. 471.

[12] Ferraris, *Bibliotheca,* art. *Annulus* (4).

[13] Barbier de Montault, *op. cit.,* Tom. I., p. 1 62.

[14] Barbier de Montault, *loc. cit.* - "*Et notandum quod novi Cardinales, etiamsi antea erant praelati, non debent portare annulos antequam habeant annulum a Summo Pontifice*" (*Rom. Cerem*). This regulation applies only to Prelates living in Rome at the time of their appointment as Cardinals.

[15] Decrees of Alexander VII. and Benedict XIV. - Pius VII., *Const. Decet Romanum Pontificem* (1823).

[16] Pius X. Const. *Inter multiplices* (1905), n. 4.

[17] Pius X. *Const. cit.,* n. 5.

[18] Pius X. *Const. cit.,* n. 27, 31 , 47, 49.

[19] Mgr. Battandier, *Annuaire Pontifical* (1906), p. 449.

[20] S. R. C., May 22, 1612 - February 13, 1625 - Nov. 20, 1628 - May 23, 1846 - June 30, 1880, etc.

[21] Pontificals Romanum, de *Consecratione electi in Episcopum.* - Durandus Mim., *Rationale,* Book III., ch. XIV. - Honorius Aug., *Opera liturgica,* Book I., ch. 216 (in Migne P. L., vol. 172, col. 609).

Chapter Three - Mitre

1. There is no documentary evidence that the mitre was in general use before the tenth century. Before that time, it seems to have been the special head-dress of the Pope and of the principal members of the clergy of Rome. In the eleventh century, certain Popes began to grant the privilege of wearing the mitre to Bishops whom they intended to honor in some special manner. [1] But the mitre does not appear in history as one of the episcopal insignia before the twelfth century. From that time on, Bishops are always represented as wearing the mitre; the bronze doors of the cathedral of Benevento, which were wrought about 1150 A. D., represent, among other subjects, the Archbishop of that city with his twenty suffragan Bishops, all wearing the mitre.

Abbots adopted the mitre in the same century, [2] in spite of the objections of some rigid observants, like St. Bernard, who inveighed against the wearing of this new ornament by Abbots, as breathing worldly vanity. But these pious protests were of no avail, and, very shortly after St. Bernard's death, the wearing of the mitre became the privilege of Abbots as well as of Bishops.

2. The essential parts of the mitre are two flat pieces terminating in point, sewed together at the lower part of their lateral sides; with two flaps, called "fanons," in Latin, *infulae, vittae,* meant to fall from it behind over the shoulders of the wearer. Originally these fanons may have been strings or strips destined to secure the mitre on the head of the Prelate by being tied under the chin.

Mitre. Note the *titulus,* the *circulus* and the arms of the Prelate embroidered on the *fanons.*

Artists and manufacturers of ecclesiastical vestments often lose sight of the traditional ornamentation of the mitre, which should essentially consist of two bands called respectively *circulus* and *titulus.* The *circulus* is a band which encircles the lower part of the mitre, so as to form a crown around the forehead of the Prelate; the *titulus* is the band which is perpendicular to the *circulus.* [3] Often, though incorrectly, a cross, or floral designs are embroidered on mitres instead of these traditional bands. In the last quarter of a century, there has been a universal movement towards the revival of the

graceful shape and traditional decoration of the medieval mitre. The mitre thus shaped was the only one in use until the end of the sixteenth century; at that time, a new form of the mitre crept into use, and was soon pretty generally adopted; it is what is known as the "seventeenth century mitre," or "Italian mitre." It is ogival in shape, a cubit long, and the *titulus* and *circulus* are in most cases omitted. This high mitre is not only ugly and out of proportion, but is heavy and inconvenient to wear. These defects have prompted many Prelates to revert to the pre-renaissance form of the mitre, the "low mitre," as it is called, which is more traditional in its shape and decoration, much less heavy, and perfectly secure on the head.

3. There are three kinds of mitres - *mitra pretiosa, mitra auriphrygiata,* and *mitra simplex.* [4]

The precious mitre (*mitra pretiosa*), as its name indicates, should be as richly adorned as possible. It is made of fine white silk or silver cloth tastefully embroidered with silk and gold, and may be studded with precious stones. On its "fanons," which end in gold tassels or fringes, the Prelate's coat-of-arms is appropriately embroidered in heraldic colors.

Precious Mitre

The orphreyed mitre (*mitra auriphrygiata*) is less rich than the *mitra pretiosa*. According to the etymology of its name, this mitre should be "embroidered with gold." Since the eighteenth century, custom seems to have prevailed to make it of plain gold cloth; but many Prelates have recently come back to the old "*auriphrygiata*," and wear it as a white silk mitre, with the titulus and circulus "applique" or embroidered with silk and gold.

The simple mitre (*mitra simplex* or *mitra simplex alba*) is entirely white, made of silk damask or linen, without embroidery, and its fanons terminate in red fringes. The simple mitre of the Pope is of silver cloth, bordered with a strip of gold. This style of mitre is a special privilege of the Sovereign Pontiff, which no other Prelate is ever allowed to wear. The simple mitre of Cardinals and Bishops is of white silk damask. When Abbots, Protonotaries and others who enjoy, by special privilege, the use of the pontificals are directed by the rubrics or the papal document to wear the simple mitre, the style of mitre meant is one of white linen with red fringes of silk to the fanons. This simple mitre of linen is also worn by Bishops, but only when they dress in their pontificals in presence of the Pope; [5] on such occasions, the simple mitre worn by Cardinals is the mitre of white silk damask. [6]

Sometimes the Ceremonial of Bishops designates the orphreyed mitre as *mitra simplex,* and the simple mitre as *mitra simplex alba;* but, in both cases, the style designated is made clear by the context.

Cardinals and Bishops may make use of the three kinds of mitres, according to the directions given by the Ceremonial. [7] Abbots are entitled to use only two mitres - the *auriphrygiata* and the *simplex alba,* [8] unless they have been granted a special privilege; and the same regulations must be observed by the seven Protonotaries Apostolic *di numero.* [9] By his constitution *Inter multiplices,* Pius X., granted to the Protonotaries Apostolic *supernumerary* the privilege of wearing a special mitre, which corresponds to the "auriphrygiata" of higher Prelates; this mitre is made of white silk, bordered with

Greek Bishop vested in his pontificals.

gold, and its fanons end in gold fringes. It is worn by the Prelate at such times as the Ceremonial directs the Bishop to put on the precious mitre. [10]

The Protonotaries Apostolic *ad instar participantium* are entitled to wear only one mitre, the simple mitre of white silk damask without any embroidery, the fanons of which end in red fringes. [11]

4. From the above principles it follows that the mitre does not exclusively belong to Bishops; therefore, expressions in which the word "mitre" is taken figuratively for "episcopate" or "diocese" are incorrect; it can not mean epis-

copate, because the mitre is not a sign of order; or, "diocese," because it is still less a sign of jurisdiction.

5. Another abuse, which is quite common in Europe - but fortunately is almost unknown in this country - consists in wearing the mitre, instead of the biretta, as a complement of the choir dress; while the mitre should be worn only when the Prelate is "paratus," that is, clad in his pontificals. [12]

6. All Prelates who are entitled by law to wear the mitre Cardinals, Bishops and Abbots should be buried with the mitre on; those who wear it by general or special privilege, as Prelates and Canons, should not be laid out and buried with the mitre on, but with the biretta. [13]

7. The mitre of Oriental Bishops is very different from that worn by the Prelates of the Western Church, for it looks like an imperial crown. This shape, which is universal in the Eastern rites, is very ancient, as we find it mentioned in the writings of Sophronius, Patriarch of Jerusalem, who died in 538. Some Oriental rites, however, have given up the use of the Eastern mitre and adopted the Occidental; such are the Maronites, Copts and Syrians. Among Armenian Bishops, there is no uniformity of usage on this point; some wearing the Latin mitre while others remain faithful to Oriental traditions. [14]

[1] St. Leo IX. in 1049, gave the "Roman mitre," with the title of Primate, to Eberhart, Archbishop of Treves. This is the first instance known of the concession of the mitre. Some other instances are recorded before this, but the texts which mention them are of doubtful authenticity.

[2] According to Mabillon, the first concession of the mitre to an abbot was made by Alexander II. in 1061. this abbot was Elgesinus, Abbot of St. Augustine s, Canterbury; but there are instances of earlier concessions.

[3] Cahier et Martin, *Nouveaux Melanges d'Archéologie* (Décoration d'églises), p. 1, seq. - Battandier, *Annuaire Pontifical* (1900), p. 185.

[4] *Caer. Episc.* I., XVII., 1.

[5] On no other occasion are Bishops supposed to wear the linen mitre.

[6] The color of the mitre is now invariably white (gold cloth standing for white). There are instances of mitres of different colors, proving that the present discipline on this point was not so strictly adhered to in ancient times. - Cfr. Woodward, *Ecclesiastical Heraldry*, p.68. - Battandier, *Annuaire* (1900), pp. 186-7 (1901), pp. 162-3.

[7] *Caer. Episc.* I., xvii., 2, 3.

[8] S. R. C., July 20, 1660.

[9] Pius X. *Const. Inter multiplices* (1906), n. 9.

[10] Pius X. *Const. cit.,* n. 27.

[11] Pius X. *Const. cit.,* n. 47.

[12] *Caer. Episc.* II., I., 4. - II., VIII., 21. - Roman Pontifical, *passim.* - In some cases, the Bishop may wear the mitre without being vested in his pontificals; it is when he performs consecrations without solemnity, or when administering confirmation privately.

[13] See chapter IX., of the same part.

[14] Battandier, *Annuaire Pontifical* (1900), pp. 198-9.

Chapter Four - Crosier

1. The crosier or pastoral staff (*baculus pastoralis*) is an ecclesiastical ornament which symbolizes the pastoral authority of Bishops and Abbots. Its symbolical meaning was felt very early in the history of the church, but its real origin is probably to be traced back to the ordinary walking sticks, which the Apostles used in their long journeys. [1]

The crosier consists of a long staff, curved at the top, and pointed at the bottom. When not in use, it may be divided into sections and kept in a box. [2]

According to strict etiquette, the crosier should be of gold or gilt silver for Cardinals and Patriarchs, and of silver for Archbishops, Bishops and Abbots; [3] but this point of discipline is seldom observed, and most crosiers are more modestly made of gilded brass.

Some authors say that Abbots belonging to the Order of the Reformed Cistercians (Trappists) should make use of a crosier of wood; but this is an exaggeration of severity, peculiar to one branch of the Order, which has no foundation in the general law of the Church or even in the traditions of the Cistercian Order; St. Bernard, the great Cistercian Abbot, founder of Clairvaux, and a strong supporter of the old monastic discipline, made use of a metallic crosier.

2. Cardinals, Prelates invested with the episcopal character, and Abbots, are entitled by law to use the crosier; and Abbesses have pretty generally usurped the same privilege. Other Prelates, who may have been granted the use of the pontificals, are not allowed that of the crosier, unless an individual exception is made. [4]

Early monuments testify that, up to the tenth century, the Roman Pontiff made use of the crosier like other Bishops. How this practice ceased is not known; but it was soon forgotten, and legendary as well as symbolical reasons were ventured in order to explain the present-day usage. One of the most commonly found is that the curved top of the crosier is a symbol of a limited jurisdiction, and, therefore, can not suit the Pope, whose jurisdiction is universal. [5]

The crosier, being a token of jurisdiction, is used by Cardinals in Rome in their titles, and every where outside of Rome; by the Apostolic Delegate, throughout the territory of his Delegation; by Archbishops, in their provinces; by

Crozier

78

Bishops, in their dioceses; and by Abbots, in their monasteries. The diocesan Bishop may allow a stranger Bishop to use the crosier in his diocese; but it is better not to do so, especially when the outsider officiates in presence of the diocesan, so as to preserve a well-marked difference between the Ordinary and the visiting Prelate. An Abbot can not lawfully use the crosier outside of his monastery, and a Bishop has not the power to grant him that privilege; [6] to do so, a Papal indult is necessary.

The proper way to carry the crosier is to hold it with the left hand at the handle, just below the knob, which connects the crook with the staff, the curve being turned forward. [7] The Prelate should not hold the crosier lifted, but alternately raise it and rest it on the floor, as he walks.

Some Ceremonials of foreign importation and antiquated scholarship teach that an Abbot in his monastery, and a Bishop when permitted to use the crosier outside of his diocese, should turn the curve backward. There never existed such regulations. The difference in the direction of the curve in the crosier of a Bishop and that of an Abbot is marked only in Heraldry, as will be mentioned in Chapter Six.

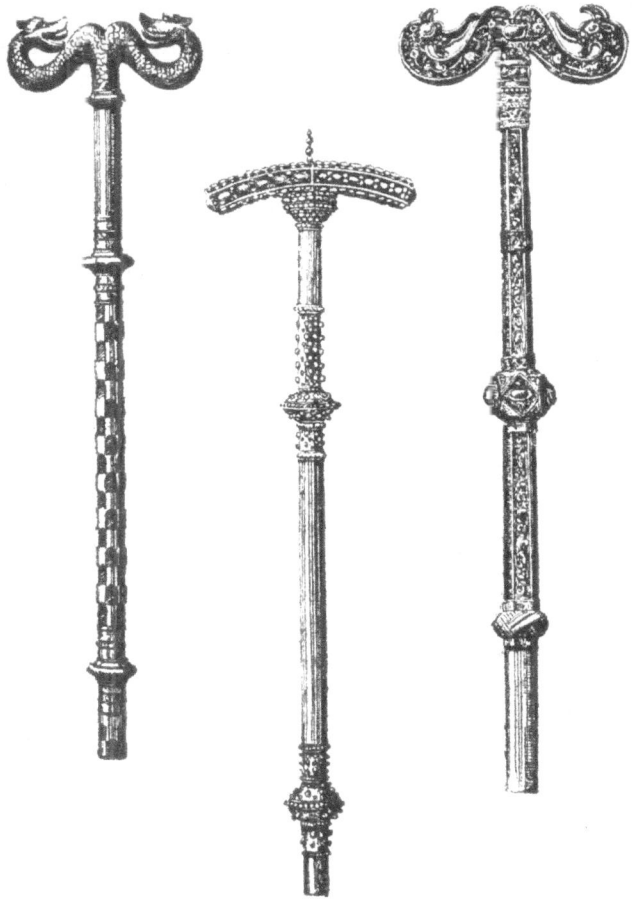

Crosiers of Oriental Bishops

Whenever a dignitary uses the crosier, whether it be by right or privilege or even without right or privilege he should always turn the curve forward. If the crosier-bearer is directed by the Ceremonial to carry the crosier so that its curve be turned backward, it is not in order to mean that he has no right to use the crosier, but in order that it be correctly turned when he hands it over to the Prelate. At processions, when the Ordinary does not carry his crosier himself, he may have it carried before him by the crosier-bearer, who, in this case, holds it raised in both hands and the curve turned forward. [8]

Cardinals and Ordinary Bishops use the crosier at High Mass, Vespers, solemn processions, and generally at all pontifical functions, except on Good Friday and at funerals. [9]

A Bishop officiating outside of his diocese, or any other Ordinary outside his jurisdiction, although forbidden the crosier at pontifical ceremonies, must nevertheless use it when performing functions in which it is required by the rubrics, such as ordinations and solemn consecrations, and, in such cases, he carries and uses the crosier throughout the ceremony, as though he were within his own jurisdiction. [10]

As was remarked for the mitre, the crosier supposes the full pontifical dress; [11] therefore, a Bishop should not use the crosier when vested in cappa magna or mozzetta. [12]

3. The crosier of Eastern Bishops is different from the Latin crosier. Instead of a crook, the top of the Oriental crosier consists in a cross in the form of a "T" (*crux decussata*). This form of the pastoral staff is exceedingly ancient, and was used not only in the Greek, but sometimes also in the Latin, Church, as is often found in the old monuments of the West. It points very distinctly to the primitive use of the staff as a support (*fulcinatorium, sustentaculum, reclinatorium*) or a walking stick. Often the arms of the "T" are twisted so as to represent two serpents opposed. [13]

[1] P. Morrisroe, Crosier (in *Catholic Encyclopedia*, IV., 515-6). - W. Smith and S. Cheetam, *Dict. of Christian Antiq.*, art. "*Pastoral Staff.*"

[2] The form, use and symbolical meaning of the crosier are indicated in the following mnemonic verses:
In bacilli forma, praesul, datur haec tibi norma,
Attrahe per curvum, medio rege, punge per imum;
Attrahe peccantes, rege justos, punge vagantes;
Attrahe, sustenta, stimula, vaga, morbida, lenta.
(Cap. *Cum venisset.* de Sacra unct.)

[3] Barbier de Montault, *Le costume et les usages ecclésiastiques,* II., 308.

[4] Marquis de Ségur, *Vie de Mgr. de Ségur,* I., 280.

[5] Another well-known reason is thus given by Pope Innocent III.: "The Roman Pontiff does not use the pastoral staff because St. Peter the Apostle sent his staff to Eucharius, the first bishop of Treves, whom he appointed with Valerius and Maternus to preach the Gospel to the German race. He was succeeded in his bishopric by Maternus, who was raised from the dead by the staff of St. Peter. The staff is, down to the present day, preserved with great veneration by the church of Treves." - (Innocent III., de *Sacro Altaris Mysterio,* I., 62. - Migne, P. L., ccxvii., col. 796). - St. Peter must have repeated more than once the sacrifice of his pastoral staff, for several places claim to have it.

[6] S. R. C., Sept. 27, 1659.

[7] *Caer. Episc.* II., viii., 62.

[8] *Caer. Episc.* I., xvii., 6.

[9] *Caer. Episc.* (*passim*).

[10] *Caer. Episc.* I., xvii., 5. - On such occasions, the Pope uses the ferula, a

long staff or sceptre with a cross at its top. This cross is not triple-armed, as is often believed and represented, but is an ordinary cross pattée.

[11] *Mitra et bacillus in episcopo sunt correlativa* (*Caer. Episc.* I., xvii., 3).

[12] *Caer. Episc.* II., H., 11.

[13] Cahier et Martin, *Mélanges d'archéologie*, IV., 152, seq. - Battandier, *Annuaire Pontifical* (1898, p. 110-1; 1900, p. 291-2).

Chapter Five - Other Pontificals

Four other "pontificals", the *hand-candlestick,* the two *tunicles,* the *gremial* and the *morse,* are grouped in this chapter, as the ceremonial prescriptions concerning the material, shape and use of these four insignia, are not sufficiently important to justify a separate study.

Hand-Candlestick

1. The hand-candlestick, called by rubrics and ceremonials *bugia, palmatoria* or *scotula,* is a low candlestick, with a long handle. It is held near the book by one of the attendants of the Prelate when ever the latter reads or sings something from the book. [1]

According to the Ceremonial, it should be made of gold or gilt silver for Cardinals and Patriarchs, and of silver for all other Prelates; but this distinction is seldom observed in practice.

The Pope does not make use of the hand-candle stick; the Bishop Assistant at the Pontifical Throne, who acts as candle-bearer to the Pope, holds instead an ordinary wax candle.

Hand-Candlestick

Until 1905, only Prelates invested with the episcopal character and those who enjoyed the privilege of the *pontificals* were allowed to use the hand-candlestick. Others who used it did so in virtue of personal indults.

Pope Pius X. by his Constitution *Inter multiplices* (1905) granted all Prelates, even Titular Protonotaries Apostolic (and thereby the Vicars General and Administrators of vacant dioceses, if they are not Prelates otherwise) to use the hand-candlestick not only at High Mass, but also at Low Mass celebrated with some solemnity, at Vespers and other offices, provided they do not officiate in presence of another Prelate invested with a higher dignity. [2]

Tunicles

2. When a Prelate celebrates Pontifical Mass, he wears under the chasuble the proper vestments of the Subdeacon and Deacon the tunic and the dalmatic, in order to symbolize the fulness of the three sacred orders which he possesses. The nomenclature of prelatial insignia designates these two vestments as the *tunicles;* but the rubrics of the Ceremonial of Bishops appropriately distinguish them as *tunicella* and *dalmatica.* [3]

They are made of silk, and cut like the corresponding vestments of the Subdeacon and Deacon, but somewhat shorter, reaching a little above the knees, and without lining, in order not to inconvenience the Prelate by too much weight of clothing. The *tunicella* should be a little longer and have narrower sleeves than the *dalmatica;* both are slit at the sides from the lower hem up to the sleeve, but the sleeves should not be slit, still less entirely cut out, as is sometimes done.

The tunicles should fit around the neck, the shoulder line being slit from the neck to allow the easy insertion of the head, and the ends of the slits near the neck provided with two silk ribbons which the attendants tie after having put the vestment on the Prelate. [4] The ornamentation, in front and back, consists of two narrow vertical stripes running from the shoulders to the hem, united near the bottom by two cross-stripes; the side-slits, the bottom of the vestment and the ends of the sleeves are bordered with a strip of braid. All these ornaments are appropriately of gold for Cardinals, Bishops and Abbots, of silk for lower Prelates and Canons.

The color of the tunicles is that required by the office of the day, except on *Gaudete* and *Laetare* Sundays, when purple tunicles may be worn under the rose-colored chasuble; and it may not be useless to note that black tunicles, not purple, must be used at the Pontifical Requiem Mass.

Gremial

3. The word *gremial,* in Latin, *gremiale,* means an apron. It is a square or oblong cloth which the Prelate officiating at the throne or at the faldstool wears over his lap when seated during Pontifical Mass. The gremial has no other purpose than to prevent the Prelate's hands, resting on his knees, from soiling the chasuble, hence it is not to be used at any other ceremony. [5]

The gremial is made of silk, lined and suitably embroidered; often the centre piece is a cross, but that is not necessary; the Prelate's coat-of-arms may be embroidered in the centre or at the four corners. As it is not regarded as a vestment, it requires no blessing, but it must be of the color proper for the Mass of the day, like the chasuble and the other pontifical vestments. Its proportions should be generous, about three feet in length and a little less in width, and it needs no ribbons or cords, for no rubric directs to tie it on the Prelate or to his chair.

For certain special ceremonies, like the offering of the candles at ordinations, the blessing of the holy oils, the distribution of blessed candles, ashes and palms, and the unctions at the ordination of priests or the consecration of a Bishop, the ceremonial directs the officiating Prelate to wear a washable gremial of linen, that is a simple cloth, like a napkin, edged with embroidery or lace, of the same dimensions as the silk gremial. This linen gremial, having for its sole purpose to prevent the oil, candle grease, ashes or dirt from dropping on the Prelate's vestments, its use is not restricted to the celebration of Pontifical Mass, but may be extended to whenever occasion requires. [6]

Morse

4. The *morse,* which is given in Latin documents the various names of *fibula, firmale, formale, morsus, pectorale,* and *rationale,* is a metallic clasp for the cope. [7] Nowadays, most of our copes are unduly ornamented with some sort of a clasp; but, strictly speaking, the cope should be fastened with a flap. The morse is habitually hooked on that flap.

The morse is a pontifical ornament, the use of which is reserved for the Pope, Cardinals and the Ordinary, [8] and is regarded as such an exclusive sign of jurisdiction that the Ordinary must not wear it in presence of a greater Prelate or outside his territory. It is made of gold or silver, more or less decorated with jewels or enamel, and has on the reverse side one or several hooks which serve to fasten it on the flap of the cope.

[1] No Prelate may use the hand-candlestick at the ceremonies on Good Friday. - *Caer. Episc.,* II., xxv., 13. - S. C. R., July 30, 1910.
[2] See text in Appendix.
[3] *Caer. Episc.,* II., viii., 18.

[4] *Caer. Episc.,* II., VIII., 18.
[5] *Caer. Episc.,* I., xi., 9.
[6] *Caer. Episc.,* II., xvi., 3. - II., xviii., 1. - II., xxi., 6.
[7] *Caer. Episc.,* II., i., 4.
[8] S. R. C., Sept. 15., 1753.

Chapter Six - Heraldry

1. Heraldry may be defined as the art, practice or science of recording genealogies, blazoning arms or armorial ensigns, and also of devising coats-of-arms. It is said also to be the science which teaches one how to blazon, that is, describe a coat-of-arms in proper technical terms. [1]

Heraldry is a science, inasmuch as it lays down correct principles, and draws conclusions which properly flow from them.

Since Prelates use armorial ensigns, it will be useful to lay down some practical rules for guidance in their selection. [2]

2. A coat-of-arms being a privilege of nobility, [3] Bishops, and Prelates bear one, for they are regarded as noble.

The episcopal character of Bishops, the eminent dignity of Cardinals, even if they are not of noble descent, places them on a par with the "rulers of this world." By their appointment to this high position, they take rank among the; "princes of the people," a rank which has never been called in question.

The offices of the Prelates of the Roman Court were formerly reserved for persons of noble birth. At present, though the above rule is far from being so absolute, these dignities, however, remain "noble offices." Therefore, Roman etiquette, faithful to tradition, requires that such Prelates as have no hereditary right of bearing arms prepare for themselves an escutcheon, if not as a sign of nobility, at least as a symbol of high dignity and prelatical functions. In this way, all Prelates appear equal, and there is no external distinction between Prelates who are of noble birth and those who are not.

Since Bishops and Prelates have an escutcheon bearing their *arms,* it may prove interesting to know how to explain these arms, and also, occasionally, to known how to compose a coat-of-arms without sinning against the rules of heraldry. To avoid mistakes, it is well to start out with the principle that a coat-of-arms is not and needs not be symbolical. [4] A coat-of-arms is only a distinct personal mark or sign. Any or every sort of drawing can not be used as a heraldic bearing; it must conform to the laws of Heraldry in regard to shape, colors, disposition, etc.; but a "meaning" is not necessary. Asking the "meaning" of a coat-of-arms is a sure sign of heraldic ignorance, and scarcely any question can be more irritating to a scholarly herald.

3. Heraldic bearings are called "arms," because they were first worn at war and tournaments by military men, who had them painted on their shields and embroidered on their banners. They are also called "coats-of-arms" from the custom of the mediaeval knights to have them embroidered on the coats they wore over their armors.

Among the different sorts of *arms,* those of Prelates, in this country, may be "arms of family, if the Prelate has inherited them, or "assumptive arms, if he adopts them when receiving his appointment.

The *figures,* or *charges,* that make up the coat-of-arms are represented on a field," or ground, cut in the shape of a shield, and called for that reason *shield* or *escutcheon* (in Latin, *scutum* or *stemma*), for, as is said above, these marks were originally painted on bucklers or shields. For most of these figures, there is a traditional, conventional shape, and a proportional size, which must be adhered to.

In face of the too prevailing ignorance of the true character of heraldry in general, and especially of ecclesiastical heraldry, it can not be too strongly emphasized that the shield and the figures drawn upon it form the principal part of the coat-of-arms, in fact, constitute the real coat-of-arms; all the other features which make up the heraldic "achievement", are so many accessories chiefly meant to indicate the Prelate's rank and dignity. It is not expected therefore that anything within the shield denote its owner's prelacy or symbolize his devotions, religious aspirations or program; the shield and its figures completely fulfill their purpose if they have reference to his name or family or, at least, sufficiently distinguish him from any other of his colleagues.

English heraldry has a peculiar *vocabulary*, chiefly derived from the old French, owing to the fact that heraldry was developed in England especially after the conquest of that country, by William, Duke of Normandy. The terms used in heraldry may be easily found in manuals treating of that matter, and in dictionaries and cyclopaedias under the heading "Heraldry."

The various *colors* of arms, which are common both to shields and their bearings, are called *tinctures*. There are ordinarily but seven tinctures in armory, of which two are *metals* the other five are *colors*.

The metals are: Gold, termed *Or,* and Silver, termed *Argent.*

The colors are: *Azure* (blue), *Gules* (red), *Vert* or *Sinople* (green). *Sable* (black), and *Purpure* (purple). *Purpure* is very seldom used. English heraldry admits two other colors, viz.: *Tenny* (orange) and *Sanguine* (blood-color); but, they are to be found only in British bearings, and even there but rarely.

Engravers should not ignore the fact that since the sixteenth century there is a conventional system of dots and lines to represent the tinctures in monochrome engravings and drawings. This system is universally adopted and must necessarily be used; otherwise it is impossible to know from a black drawing what are the colors of the bearings. The system is this:

Or (gold) is represented by dots.

Argent (silver) needs no mark and is, therefore plain.

Azure (blue) is represented by horizontal lines

Gules (red), by perpendicular lines.

Vert (green), by diagonal lines from *dexter* to *sinister*. [5]

Purpure (purple), by diagonal lines from *sinister* to *dexter*.

Sable (black), by horizontal and perpendicular lines crossing each other (a combination of *Azure* and *Gules*).

Tenny (orange), by diagonal lines from *sinister* to *dexter,* crossed by horizontal lines (a combination of *Purpure* and *Azure*).

Sanguine (blood-color), by diagonal lines crossing each other from *dexter* to *sinister* and *vice versa* (a combination of *Vert* and *Purpure*).

Besides the metals and the colors, several *furs* are used as tinctures, those most generally used being *ermine* and *vair*. Ermine is white, with black spots of conventional shape. The reverse of *ermine,* that is, white spots on a black field, is known as *ermines. Vair* is expressed with blue and white skins, cut into the form of little bells ranged in rows and opposite to each other, the base of the white being always next to that of the blue. When the base of the blue pieces is next to that of other blue pieces, the fur thus represented is called *counter-vair*. If other colors than blue and white are used, they must be expressed, this way, for instance: "Vairy Or and Gules."

British heraldry has adopted a certain number of other furs which are not used in other nations.

The plate illustrating these principles gives, on the right side of each "tinctured" shield, its equivalent in black, thus showing how easy it is to represent, in a monochrome design, all the different tinctures of a real shield of arms. Anyone may, with the help of these few principles, readily find out the actual colors of all heraldic bearings properly designed.

A rule too often violated in making a coat-of-arms for a Prelate, is that *"color should never be used upon color, or metal upon metal"*; but *furs* may be used both upon colors and upon metals. Violations of this rule may sometimes be found in hereditary armorials, the possessors of which invariably allege some fabulous, if always honorable, reasons for such violations. Upon close study, however, a heraldic scholar will usually find that the so-called "honorable exception" simply results from an initial error of composition.

The foregoing rule does not apply however to small accessories like the *langue* (tongue) of lions, the talons of the birds of prey, etc. Also, when the field is equally compounded of color and metal (as "barry", "bendy", "paly", etc.), the charges over all may be a color or metal, if it be different from those used on the field; and, on a plain field, a charge may be used that is equally compounded of color and metal, if both differ from the tincture of the field.

An important principle is that the simplest *arms* are the best. Complicated bearings are often difficult to read, draw or engrave, and the number of charges being greater, the chances of error are thereby multiplied. The most ancient bearings are as a rule very simple, and the modern composer must adhere to that tradition of simplicity, if he wishes to obtain truly artistic results. Few persons indeed are really capable of composing a correct coat-of-arms; and an incorrect coat-of-arms is, in the eyes of the man who knows heraldry, something not less ridiculous than a page written in pretentious style but full of mispellings. Therefore, when a Prelate chooses heraldic bearings, he should take care to have his arms designed by some person thoroughly acquainted with the principles of heraldic composition.

Before concluding these general principles, a word must be said of the *motto* which many persons seem to regard as the principal part in an armorial achievement. The *motto* has little importance: it is a late innovation, for it does not date further back than the sixteenth century; and ecclesiastical heraldry has not known it until the first years of the nineteenth, when its popularity grew in proportion to the general ignorance of the principles of sound heraldry. In Rome, where good traditions are preserved in this matter, the *motto* finds no place in the arms of Prelates. At any rate, the *motto*, if used should not be written upon the shield, but placed below it on a scroll.

4. The shield and its charges are essentially personal and independent of their owner's Prelacy, so that they remain identical throughout the Prelate's career, no matter what promotions he may obtain; the only mutable part of the achievement, which is altered when the Prelate's rank is changed, is entirely outside the shield, and is made up of what the manuals of heraldry term "external ornaments", that is, certain tokens of ecclesiastical dignity which

are traditionally accepted as meaning the rank of each Prelate in the sacred hierarchy, such as the pontifical hat, the cross, the crosier and the mitre.

Formerly an ancient and almost universally accepted custom allowed Prelates who were in possession of a personal title of nobility or were members of secular orders of knighthood to ornament their shields of arms not only with the usual prelatial insignia, but also with the coronets or other marks of honor befitting their titles, and the decorations of the knightly orders. This custom was abolished for Cardinals in 1644, by Pope Innocent X. [6] and the prohibition was extended, in 1915, to Patriarchs, Archbishops and Bishops by a decree of the Sacred Consistorial Congregation, issued by command of Pope Benedict XV. This decree forbids Prelates invested with the episcopal character to use in the external ornamentation of their coats-of-arms any personal insignia of a secular dignity or any decoration of a knightly order,

except the Order of St. John of Jerusalem ("Order of Malta") and the Order of the Holy Sepulchre. [7] The purpose of these excellent regulations is to establish a wholesome personal equality among Cardinals and Bishops.

Arms of a Cardinal not invested with the episcopal character.

The Holy See, however, recognizes in this document that certain bishoprics have, by virtue of a long possession, acquired the right to preserve the use or memory of special honors which have been added to them in the course of ages; if, therefore, a title of nobility or some other secular distinction is attached to a Bishop's see, he has the right to decorate his arms with whatever external ornaments symbolize the special illustration of his bishopric. Archiepiscopal and episcopal sees in this country are of too recent foundation to have acquired any such distinctions, so that our Cardinals, Archbishops and Bishops must decorate their shields with no other external insignia than the regular marks of Prelacy allowed by ecclesiastical heraldry and regulated as follows.

Cardinals place over their shields the pontifical red hat, [8] with its scarlet strings, tastefully intertwined, symmetrically hanging on each side of the shield, and ending with fifteen tassels disposed in five rows. If the Cardinal is invested with the episcopal character, he places behind the shield a gold cross, the foot of which is visible at the bottom of the shield, and the arms and head over it. If the Cardinal is, or was, an Archbishop, custom allows him to place there a double-armed cross.

This cross is not an ornament fixed on the top of the shield, but it is supposed to represent the cross which is borne before an Archbishop in processions, and should be designed as placed behind the shield. When the shield is colored, the cross is painted in gold.

Formerly, this double cross was the proper mark of the Patriarchal dignity, and Archbishops placed behind their shields an ordinary processional cross of gold, while Bishops who do not make use of the cross in processions and liturgical functions did not place it in their bearings. But about the seventeenth century, Archbishops began to place in their arms the double cross; and Bishops, the ordinary cross which was hitherto reserved for Archbishops. This practice has now become universal. It is to be noted, however, that the double cross, with which Archbishops "timber" their arms,

Arms of a Cardinal who is, at the same time, an Archbishop.

does not signify that they possess the right of having such a cross carried before them in processions. The cross which is borne before a Metropolitan Archbishop does not differ in shape from the ordinary processional cross; and Archbishops, who are not Metropolitans, though privileged to timber their arms with the double cross, do not make use of the archiepiscopal cross in liturgical functions. [9]

The arms of a Patriarch are timbered with the double cross and the green pontifical hat, with its strings terminating in fifteen tassels on each side, disposed in five rows. [10]

The ornaments of an Archbishop's arms are the same as those of a Patriarch s; but the green pontifical hat has only ten tassels on each side, disposed

Arms of an Archbishop.

in four rows. Under the hat, and passed behind the shield, is seen the double cross, now a sign of the archiepiscopal dignity.

Bishops place be hind their shields an ordinary processional cross of gold, surmounted by the green pontifical hat, with its green strings, each terminating in six tassels, disposed in three rows. [11]

The Prelates of the Roman Court who are not invested with the episcopal character are not entitled to timber their arms with the cross or with the mitre, though they may have the privilege of wearing the latter during certain ceremonies; but they are free to place over the shield the coronet significative of their title of nobility (if they have one), and, at any rate, the pontifical hat of the same shape and with the same style of strings and tassels as that of Prelates belonging to the episcopal order, the color, however, being different, as is indicated in the following paragraphs.

The four Prelates *di fiochetti* [12] - the Vice-Camerlengo of the Roman Church, the Auditor-General and the Treasurer-General of the Reverend Chamber Apostolic and the Majordomo of His Holiness - are privileged to place over their shields a purple pontifical hat, with rose-colored, or, rather, amaranth red, strings, each ending in ten tassels of the same color, disposed like those of the Archbishop's hat.

Protonotaries Apostolic have the privilege of the same purple hat, with the same red strings and tassels, but the tassels are only six in number on each side, and disposed in three rows.

All other Domestic Prelates timber their arms with a purple pontifical hat, from which hang two purple strings, each ending with six purple tassels disposed m three rows like those of the Bishop's hat.

Arms of a Bishop.

Arms of a Prelate "di fiochetti."

"Black Protonotanes," Vicars General, Abbots, Superiors General of Religious Orders and Congregations, and all priests having a permanent and extensive Ordinary jurisdiction, timber their escutcheons with a hat of the same shape and with the same arrangement of strings and tassels as that of Bishops and Domestic Prelates; but, the hat, its strings and its tassels are black, even when the religious habit of the dignitary is of a different color.

The hat which the Prelates *di mantellone* should place over their arms is purple, with purple strings ending in three tassels disposed in two rows. Often they use the same hat as the Domestic Prelates, but such practice is not in accordance with the present rules of etiquette.

Outside of Italy, there is a very general practice, which consists in ornamenting the shields of Archbishops, Bishops and Abbots, with the crosier and the mitre. This practice is nearly universal, and is even more ancient than the regulations concerning the use of the heraldic hat. When, in the sixteenth century, the Roman custom of placing the pontifical hat above the shield became general, the old fashion was retained inasmuch as the hat was placed above the crosier and mitre. The rubrics of the Pontifical for the consecration of a Bishop evidence some uncertainty as to this point of heraldic usage, thus showing that, at the time of the revision of the Roman Pontifical, there was no uniformity of practice. [13]

The heraldic use of the crosier and mitre may be retained, as there is no legal text against it; yet it might be advisable, for greater perfec-

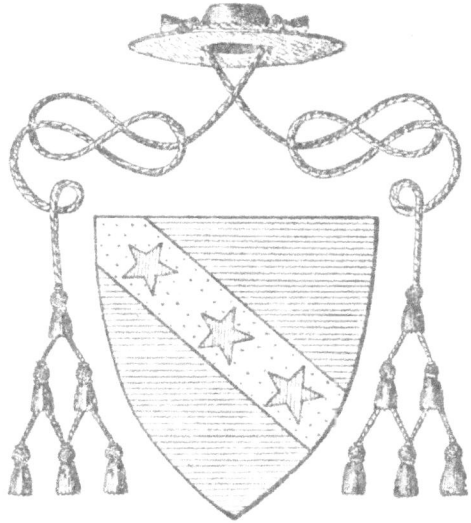

Arms of a Protonotary Apostolic, of a Domestic Prelate, Vicar General, Superior General, etc. Note that the only difference is in the color of the hat.

Arms of a Prelate *di mantellone* (purple hat), and of a Canon (black hat).

tion, to conform with the Roman usage. If, however, the old practice is retained, it should be in accordance with the accepted principles of ecclesiastical heraldry; therefore the mitre should not be placed in the middle, between the cross and the crosier; but the cross should be placed in the middle, the mitre on the left (*dexter*) and the crosier on the right (*sinister*). Like the cross, the crosier should be represented as placed behind the shield.

Abbots do not place a cross behind the shield, since this is a privilege of Prelates invested with the episcopal character; but they may place, below the pontifical hat, the crosier passed behind the right side of the shield, and the mitre resting on the top of the shield on the left side; or simply, as is done in Rome, the crosier in the middle.

In the case of Archbishops and Bishops, the curve of the crosier is turned towards the right; while in the arms of Abbots, it is turned towards the left.

All priests who have a permanent appointment, like Canons, irremovable Rectors of parishes, etc., may timber their arms with a hat.

Arms of an Abbot.

This hat is shaped like that of Prelates, but is of no other color than black, and its strings terminate with three tassels on each side for Canons, and one tassel only for other dignitaries.

The clerical members and officials of any Order of Knighthood are entitled to use its ribbon and badge as an external ornament of their shield of arms. If they belong to the lower classes of the Order, and so are only entitled to wear the ribbon and badge at the buttonhole, or on the left breast - then the cross is suspended by its ribbon from the base of the shield. But if they have higher rank, which entitles them to wear the ribbon *en sautoir* - that is by a ribbon passing round the neck and supporting the badge at the neck or middle of the breast - then they have also the right to surround the escutcheon with the ribbon of the Order supporting its pendant badge, and (according to circumstances) to place their escutcheon upon the Cross of the Order." [14]

This general principle, quoted from a scholarly author, remains true for ordinary clergymen and lower Prelates, but no longer applies to Cardinals, Patriarchs, Archbishops and Bishops, except in regard to the insignia of two Orders which have retained a religious character, namely, the Order of Malta and the Order of the Holy Sepulchre. [15]

Books dealing with Heraldry may give different rules concerning the various points here treated, especially concerning the colors of hats and the number of their tassels; but they are either ill-informed or antiquated. The directions here given are all in conformity with the present ceremonial of the Roman Church, and are, therefore, to be preferred to the teaching of heralds, who may know secular heraldry very well, but are often imperfectly acquainted with ecclesiastical etiquette.

Few heraldic treatises mention the immemorial custom according to which Cardinals, Archbishops and Bishops belonging to Religious Orders should signal that membership by uniting their personal arms with those of the Order. This may be heraldically done in two ways; either the arms of the Order contain as the main figure an oblong object which can be stretched in height, in which case the Prelate "impales" his own arms with those of his Order in the same shield, giving the place of honor, *dexter,* to the Order; or the Order arms have for principal figure a round object or one which can be stretched in width, in which case, the Order arms are placed "in chief" above the Prelate's individual coat. In both cases, the two coats thus combined form a real heraldic unit the two parts of which however could be easily separated should the Prelate's membership in the Order happen to cease. Hence the two elements should never be so mixed that they could not be separated without losing their individual character.

The custom of "impaling" the arms of a corporation is one which has been known and practiced for centuries in the English speaking episcopate. A residential Archbishop or Bishop impales his own arms with those of his dio-

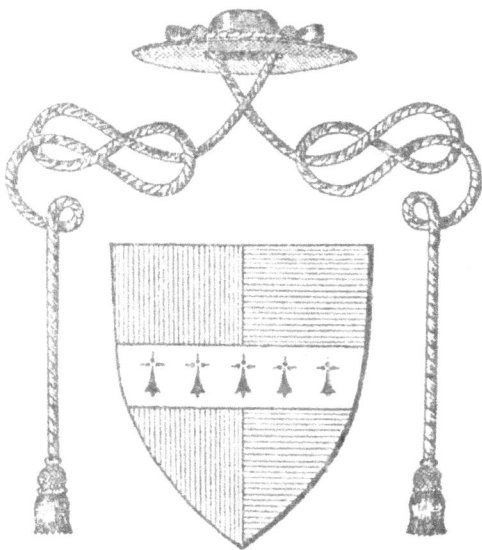

Arms of a priest having a permanent appointment.

A Bishop's official seal.

cese, giving the *dexter* side to the diocese, so that the official arms of an Ordinary really contain two coats united side by side in the same shield. When the Prelate is transferred to another see, his own side of the shield remains unchanged, but he impales on the *dexter* side the arms of his new bishopric. Should he happen to resign his jurisdiction, then the figures composing his coat-of-arms ought to be spread so as to occupy the whole surface of the shield. This method, which is quite generally followed in this country, has the advantage of creating a singular continuity in the arms of Prelates who governed the same diocese, and permits to distinguish at a first glance the coat-of-arms of an Ordinary from that of a Titular Bishop.

A Bishop's private seal.

Outside of English speaking countries, this combination of coats is rarely resorted to, and it is practically unknown in Italy. In other places, particularly in Germany and Switzerland, the combination is usually made by "quartering", instead of "impaling"; but an explanation of this different method would go far beyond the modest limits allotted to this elementary chapter.

5. The uses of the prelatial coat-of-arms are many and various.

The coat-of-arms is a personal, distinctive sign of a Prelate, both as a dignitary of the Church and a distinguished private citizen. From this principle all its practical uses are derived.

Prie-dieu with the coat-of-arms embroidered on the drapery

First of all, the coat-of-arms constitutes the principal part of the Prelate's seal. A Prelate invested with a permanent office, like a Cardinal, a Bishop, a Secretary of a Congregation, etc., has at least two different seals; one, the official seal, is made up of the coat-of-arms rounded with the name and titles of the Prelate, in Latin, and in abbreviation if necessary; for instance, "FRAN-CISCUS. S. R. E. PRESB. CARD. RICHARD. ARCHIEP. PARISIEN." or "PETRUS. EPISC. TITUL. CAESARIEN." The other, much smaller, is reserved for private use, and consists only of the coat-of-arms within a circle. The Prelates who do not make use of the official seal, may well use a private seal with their arms engraved.

The terms *"arms"* and *"seal"* are often incorrectly used as synonymous. In fact, the coat-of-arms is independent of the seal, though the seal usually includes the coat-of-arms as its principal element.

As a sign of jurisdiction and authority, the coat-of-arms of a Bishop should be printed on the top of all chancery documents, like letters of ordinations, diplomas, testimonial letters, celebrets, etc. In such cases, the coat-of-arms should be of a rather large scale, and all its details neatly printed with the conventional dots and lines indicating the colors. Under the coat-of-arms, the names and the ecclesiastical titles of the Prelate are printed in full; and, at the foot of the document, at the left of the Prelate's signature, the official seal is affixed.

The Bishop's coat-of-arms is also printed, as a sign of jurisdiction or of high patronage, on the cover and title page of all diocesan publications, as a diocesan bulletin, documents printed by order of the Bishop, acts of synods, diocesan statutes, pastoral letters, conferences, etc.

In church, the canopy of the episcopal throne should be decorated with the Bishop's coat-of-arms embroidered in colors, as well as sacred vestments, chasubles, stoles, mitres, copes, etc., personally belonging to him or presented by him.

It is also a Roman usage to decorate with the embroidered coat-of-arms the front part of the drapery covering the prie-dieu of a Prelate.

In his own house, the Prelate marks with his coat-of-arms everything which belongs to him personally, and is fit to receive such a decoration his plate (both sacred and common), china, tapestries, hangings, rugs, cushions, etc. His arms should be painted on both doors of his carriage; and a wood panel, bearing the coat-of-arms painted, should be placed, as a sign of propriety and jurisdiction, over the entrance door of the Bishop's house and over the doorway of the cathedral. [16]

Finally, custom places the arms of a Prelate, printed in black or in colors, on the top of the letter paper used by him, or, in his name, by his secretaries; and the same arms, a very artistic piece of decoration as they are, should be made use of whenever it is possible to do so; for instance, on programmes, menu cards, engrossed addresses, etc., when a Prelate is interested in the occasion.

In all cases above mentioned, if the Prelate's arms are not painted, embroidered or printed in their proper heraldic colors, the conventional system of dots and lines, signifying the different tinctures of the shield and its charges, should invariably be used; but there is no law of heraldry, etiquette or good taste requiring a Cardinal's arms to be printed in solid red, or a Bishop's in purple.

[1] The general principles and practical rules given in this chapter are only the most essential, and are not intended as a treatise on Heraldry; for further study and explanation of the various technical terms, the reader should have recourse to some of the many manuals on Heraldry.

[2] Whether it [heraldry] be indeed the "noble science," as one of its enthusiastic votaries has termed it, or, as a later writer has affirmed, "the science of the fools with long memories," may be a more or less open question; but as it is guided by positive rules, which can not with impunity be violated, so long as it is employed at all, either in the restoration of old buildings, illumination, glass-painting, or any other field of art. it can only be properly employed after some little attention has been paid to requirements which, though arbitrary in their character, have received the sanction of centuries; and it is not a sufficient reason for the violation of these rules to deride the study as obsolete and absurd, for if the thing be introduced at all, it must be rightly done. (F. E. Hulme, *The History, Principles and Practice of Heraldry*, ch. I., p. 2).

[3] Throughout this chapter, the terms *noble* and *nobility* are taken in their general sense, as implying social distinction chiefly acquired by heredity; not in the restricted sense which they have in England, where *noble* and *nobility* exclusively designate persons with a *title*, namely, barons, viscounts, earls or counts, marquesses and dukes.

[4] "Heraldry appears as a science at the commencement of the thirteenth century; and although armorial bearings had then been in existence undoubtedly for some time previous, no precise date has yet been discovered for their first assumption. In their assumption the object of the assumers was not, as it had been generally asserted and believed, to symbolize any virtue or qualification, but simply to distinguish their persons and properties, to display their pretensions to certain honors or estates, attest their alliances, or acknowledge their feudal tenure." - Planché, *Pursuivant of Arms.* – "It can not be too clearly emphasized that, at a period when one warrior cased in mail, with lowered visor, was practically indistinguishable from another similarly habited, the primary, essential, function of the heraldic charges, on his shield and banner, was simply to "identify" him to his followers. And, therefore, today, if a shield of arms is so decorated with fitting heraldic forms, as to distinguish it from other shields, it fulfills the only requirement that the most exacting herald can legally demand of it, "*Arma sunt distinguendi causa.*" - Pierre de Chaignon la Rose, *Ecclesiastical Heraldry in America,* in "Christian Art," May, 1907, pp. 64-65.

[5] The shield, being supposed to be carried by a man, the right side of the drawing, as you look at it, is called *sinister* (left), and the left side is called *dexter* (right).

[6] Innocent X., Bull *Militantis Ecclesiae,* Dec. 19, 1644.

[7] *Acta Apostolicae Sedis,* Jan. 15, 1915., Vol. VII., p. 172.

[8] This hat must be of the pontifical form, that is large, with a low crown and flat brim. Designers and engravers should take care that it be in proportion with the dimensions of the shield, so as to constitute a well balanced design. The same remark applies to the hats placed over the shield of Bishops and other Prelates, for heraldic hats do not differ in form, but only in color and in the number of their tassels.

[9] Another difference between the heraldic cross and the cross carried before a Metropolitan is that the former does not bear the figure of our Lord, while the latter is a "crucifix."

[10] This is the newly-accepted etiquette on this point. Up to these last years, Patriarchs placed over their shields the same hat as Archbishops. The Patriarch of Lisbon places the tiara over his shield, but not the keys, which belong exclusively to the Pope; and even the reasons given by the Patriarchs of Lisbon for their assumption of the tiara fail to find support among historians.

[11] The "Regent of the Apostolic Chancery," though not invested with the episcopal character, has the privilege of placing over his shield a green hat similar to that of a Bishop; but since he is not Bishop, he does not place the cross behind his shield. Modern etiquette allows Abbots *nullius* the same privilege, on account of their quasi-episcopal jurisdiction.

[12] The Prelates *di fiochetti* are so called because they have the exclusive privilege of decorating the harness of their horses with purple plumes (*fiochetti*).

[13] Pont. Roman., de *Consecratione Electi in Episcopum;* "...panes et barilia ornentur...hinc et inde insignia Consecratoris et Electi habentia, cum capello, vel cruce, vel mitra, pro cuiusque gradu et dignitate".

[14] J. Woodward, *Ecclesiastical Heraldry*, pp. 56-57.

[15] *Acta Apost. Sedis*, Vol. VII., p. 172.

[16] Hac stante communi consuetudine, ac pene universali usu, insignia, arma, seu stemmata ponendi in altaribus, capellis, parietibus, turribus templorum, et in aliis locis ecclesiarum, seu etiam in ecclesiasticis ornamentis, candelabris, lampadibus, calicibus, planetis, etc., dicimus licitum esse, si quis id facit, ligitimo iure et iusto fine agat, aut, ut alios exemplo suo ad templa et altaria construenda, restauranda, vel adornanda attrahat...Episcopus non debet amovere arma, seu insignia, et monumenta, seu memorias suorum praedecessorum ab ecclesia, vel palatio episcopali, maxime si fuerunt constructa propriis ipsorum expensis. - Ferraris, *Bibliotheca Canonica*, art. *Arma*, 20.

Chapter Seven - Use of the Pontificals by Prelates Not Invested With the Episcopal Character

Some Prelates, not invested with the episcopal character, have, by law or by privilege, the right of officiating with the pontifical ceremonies and vestments, and of receiving special honors at Low Mass. Such are:

The Cardinals who have not received the episcopal consecration.

All Abbots.

The seven Protonotaries Apostolic *de numero participantium.*

The Protonotaries Apostolic *supernumerary.*

The Protonotaries Apostolic *ad instar participantium.*

The Canons of certain Basilicas and Cathedrals.

I. *Cardinals.*

Cardinals, even those who are not consecrated Bishops, have the right to officiate pontifically at the throne everywhere, except in presence of the Pope. The Ordinary of the place is bound by canon law to give up his throne to a Cardinal, unless he himself is a Cardinal.

Cardinal-Deacons, although priests in orders, according to canon 232, are not allowed to celebrate Pontifical Mass, because officially they are only Deacons; but canon 240 grants them the right to assist pontifically at Mass celebrated in their presence, and, by immemorial custom, they may publicly perform all other priestly functions with pontifical honors.

The ceremonies to be observed when a Cardinal pontificates are those prescribed by the rubrics for a Bishop having "ordinary jurisdiction".

II. *Abbots.*

Abbots and Prelates nullius have, within the limits of the territory submitted to their jurisdiction, the same right as diocesan Bishops to officiate in pontificals.

The use of the pontificals by simple Abbots is regulated by a well-known decree of the Sacred Congregation of Rites, issued September 27, 1659, by order of Pope Alexander VII., which may be summed up as follows.

An Abbot celebrating Pontifical Mass has no right to the seventh candlestick. His throne has but two steps; it is not permanently fixed, but is erected for the occasion, and its drapery and canopy should not be of costly material. The Abbot is authorized to pontificate only three times a year, and never at Requiem Mass. He is forbidden to make use of his pontificals outside of his monastery, except when invited, at a solemn funeral, to impart one of the five absolutions.

In presence of the diocesan Bishop, the Abbot officiates at a throne erected on the Epistle side; and an episcopal throne, with three steps, is erected for the Bishop, at the usual place, on the Gospel side.

At Low Mass and other offices, as well as in the administration of the sacraments, an Abbot should not differ from a simple priest, except in the wearing of the pectoral cross and the ring.

These rules bind all Abbots in general; but there have been granted very numerous privileges to individuals or communities, so that the restrictions imposed by the decree of Alexander VII. are seldom observed to the letter.

III. *Protonotaries Apostolic.*

Two decrees of Pope Pius X. have regulated the honors and insignia of Protonotaries Apostolic and other Prelates of the Roman Court. These decrees have considerably changed the hitherto vague and uncertain discipline on this point.

The first decree was issued by the S. Congregation of Rites, on March 9, 1904. Its object was to extend the privileges of the Protonotaries Apostolic on the occasion of the granting by Pope Pius X. of the title and rank of Protonotaries to the Canons of the Cathedral of Treviso, his native diocese.

The second decree (Constitution *Inter multiplices*) was a *motu proprio* of the same Pope, February 21, 1905, regulating in detail all that pertains to the dignity, rank, costume and privileges of the Prelates of the Roman Court. This second decree has some what modified the dispositions of the decree of 1904, as regards Protonotaries Apostolic.

1) *Protonotaries Apostolic de numero participantium.* - These are seven Prelates composing the College of Protonotaries. Their principal privileges are the following:

They are free to wear the *ordinary ring* at all times, even at Low Mass and at other Church Ceremonies.

They are permitted to celebrate High Mass at the faldstool with the same ceremonies as are to be observed by a Bishop celebrating Pontifical Mass outside of his jurisdiction; with the restriction, however, that they are forbidden to say *Pax vobis* after *Gloria in excelsis,* and *Sit nomen Domini* and *Adiutorium nostrum* before giving the blessing to the people. The blessing they impart is that of a priest with a single sign of the cross; but they are permitted to sing it. In presence of the Ordinary, they must abstain from giving the blessing.

In Rome, they are not permitted to celebrate pontifically, but they have the right to do so elsewhere with the permission of the Ordinary of the place.

When going to the church where they are to pontificate, they are vested in purple cassock, rochet and purple mantelletta, & wear the pectoral cross suspended from a cord of amaranth red silk, entwined with gold. They may be received at the door of the church by a master of ceremonies and two clerics.

The mitres which they use during Mass are the *auriphrygiata* and the *simple mitre* of white silk damask.

When celebrating Low Mass on some solemn occasion, they may make the preparation and thanksgiving, vested in their prelatical habit, and kneeling on a prie-dieu which should not be draped, but furnished with two purple cushions. They vest at the foot of the altar, and may be assisted by a cleric in sacred Orders and two other inferior ministers. They make use of the canon, hand-candlestick, ewer, basin and towel.

At daily Low Mass, they do not differ from other priests, except that they are allowed to wear the ring and to use the candlestick.

Their privilege of pontificating is not restricted to Mass, but extends to all pontifical offices which do not require the episcopal character.

2) *Protonotaries Apostolic Supernumerary.* - Their privileges are much less extensive than those of the members of the preceding class.

They are not allowed to wear the ordinary ring, but wear the *pontifical ring* when officiating pontifically.

Like the Protonotaries *de numero,* they may officiate at the faldstool at High Mass, Vespers, and other functions which do not require the episcopal character; but only with the explicit permission of the Ordinary, who is free to refuse the favor or to determine the days on which the Prelate may use his privilege.

In pontificating, they are bound to observe the following restrictions:-

No embroidery is allowed on their gloves, sandals and stockings, which may be bordered with a gold strip.

The pectoral cross must be of plain gold without gems, and suspended from a cord of amaranth red silk.

The pontifical ring has but one gem.

The mitres, which they use at Mass, are a special white mitre of silk, bordered with gold, and the simple mitre of linen, alternately, as is indicated in the Ceremonial of Bishops.

They wash their hands only once, at *Lavabo.*

They do not say *Pax vobis,* or impart the blessing like Bishops, but sing the form of the priest's blessing, *Benedicat vos omnipotens Deus,* etc.

When celebrating in presence of the Ordinary, they use only the linen mitre, do not give the blessing, and stand head uncovered when the Ordinary goes through the sanctuary. The same regulations hold good when the Protonotary officiates in presence of a Prelate superior to the Ordinary, as, for instance, the Metropolitan or a Cardinal.

In Rome and elsewhere, when celebrating Low Mass with some solemnity, they may make the preparation and thanksgiving before the altar, vested in their prelatic habit, without the pectoral cross and the ring, kneeling on an undraped prie-dieu, furnished with two purple cushions. They vest at the foot of the altar; may be assisted by a cleric in major Orders and two other minor clerics, and use the canon, candlestick, ewer, basin and towel. But they do not wash their hands after Communion.

At ordinary Low Mass, they do not differ from other priests, except in the use of the candlestick.

3) *Protonotaries Apostolic ad instar participantium.* - This class of Protonotaries is the only one having representatives in this country.

All that concerns their costume has been treated above in the different chapters dealing with the costume of the Prelates *di mantelletta.*

Like all Prelates and Canons, they have, in choir, the right to be incensed with two swings of the censer, to receive the blessing standing, and to bow, instead of genuflecting, to the cross of the altar.

Their right of precedence is the same as that of the Protonotaries Apostolic *supernumerary;* as such, they rank before all Clerics, Priests, Canons, Dignitaries of Chapters and Superiors of Religious Orders who have not the privilege of the pontificals. But they rank after the Vicar General of the diocese, Abbots, and the Chapter of the Cathedral.

Outside of Rome, with the permission of the Ordinary, and the consent of the Superior of the church, if the church is "exempt," they may celebrate Pontifical Mass, on such days and occasions as may be determined by the Ordinary. [1] They are never permitted to pontificate at Requiem Mass.

Their right of pontificating is the same as that of the Protonotaries Apostolic *supernumerary,* limited, however, by the following restrictions:

They are not permitted to sit on the faldstool, nor to make use of the gremial. They sit on the bench, as other priests do at High Mass. Their gloves, sandals and stockings are not embroidered, but bordered with a strip of yellow silk.

They use only one mitre - the *simple mitre* - of white silk damask, with red fringes to the fanons.

Besides a Deacon and a Subdeacon, they may have an Assistant Priest in cope; but they are not entitled to that honor if they pontificate in a Cathedral Church, or in presence of the Ordinary or of a Prelate superior to the Ordinary.

When officiating pontifically, they never let down the tram of the cassock.

They wear a plain pectoral cross without gems, suspended from a cord of purple silk. [2]

They read or sing nothing at the bench.

They wash their hands only once, at *Lavabo.*

They do not say *Pax vobis,* and they sing the ordinary blessing of a priest, which they impart with a single sign of the cross.

When going from the altar to the bench, and *vice versa,* while sitting, washing their hands, being incensed, and giving the blessing, they wear the mitre.

If they pontificate in presence of the Ordinary or of a greater Prelate, they do not give the blessing, and they stand, head uncovered, while the higher Prelate is standing or walking.

With the permission of the Ordinary, they may celebrate Pontifical Vespers, but sitting on the bench, and not giving the blessing at the end. They may also use their pontificals when giving the benediction of the Blessed Sacrament; at solemn processions; and at solemn funerals, if they are called upon to give one of the five absolutions. For all these functions, the special authorization of the Ordinary, and the permission of the Superior of the church, if the church is "exempt," are, of course, required.

In Rome, when they celebrate Low Mass with some solemnity, they enjoy the same privileges as the Protonotanes Apostolic *supernumerary.* Outside of Rome, they enjoy these privileges when commissioned by the Ordinary to say a Low Mass on some solemn occasion.

At their ordinary High Masses, and at Low Masses celebrated publicly, they may use the hand-candlestick.

IV. *Canons.*

When Canons have obtained the concession of the pontificals, they must observe the rules laid down for the Protonotanes Apostolic *ad instar participantium*; unless special dispositions are contained in the indult of concession.

No Protonotary Apostolic or Canon should be buried with his mitre on; nor should the mitre be placed on his coffin at his funeral.

These dignitaries are also prohibited from placing the mitre over their coats-of-arms.

[1] There is a current opinion that Protonotaries have a right to pontificate four times a year; but this opinion is unfounded. The Protonotary may pontificate as often as it pleases the Ordinary, but never without the consent of the Ordinary.
[2] On account of the pectoral cross which they wear, they should not cross the stole, when vesting for Pontifical Mass.

Chapter Eight - Synthetic Description of the Various Costumes of Prelates

After the various portions of a Prelate's costume, as well as the insignia which denote his proper rank in the sacred hierarchy, have been described one by one in the preceding pages, it becomes possible to work out a synthesis of the prelatial dress, by defining the several complete costumes prescribed by the Ceremonial for each class of Prelates, reserving for the following chapter the special directions as to which of these costumes is to be worn on each given occasion. But, before coming to this point, it may not be unnecessary to clear the ground by disposing of a certain number of common errors.

1. This study may well begin with the frequently asked question as to which is the "episcopal color". In spite of several authoritative pronouncements and articles in Catholic publications, many persons still believe that the episcopal color *par excellence* is purple, and some will add that they cannot understand why simple *Monsignori* should dress like Bishops. History readily disposes of this last difficulty by showing that the converse is true, namely that it is the Bishops who dress like the *Monsignori!* The Prelates of the Roman Court wore purple clothes, as members of the Pope's household, long before any Bishop thought of habitually dressing in that color. The councils of the middle-ages, legislating upon ecclesiastical dress, prescribed a dark color (*pullus color*) for the cassocks of priests and other lower clergy, reserving undetermined *bright colors* for the use of dignitaries. In accordance with these decrees, Bishops, before the sixteenth century, generally dressed in *green,* for the simple reason that, before the modern progress in chemistry, the green dye was the best and most easily obtainable. However, as a consequence of increasing facilities, in the lower middle-ages, for the importation of Oriental goods, other colors were not infrequently used; certain Bishops wore purple, others some varieties of red or a blueish violet, even a sort of deep orange or reddish brown was occasionally found. All these colors were perfectly legitimate, since Canon Law did not prescribe uni-

formity in this matter; still the marked prevalence of *green* caused this color to be regarded as the *episcopal color,* and so it has remained to this day.

For different reasons, the chief of which undoubtedly is the then prevailing influence throughout Europe of Italian art, literature and manners, the purple dress of Roman Prelates became, in the sixteenth century, the fashion among Bishops, so that the publication of the Ceremonial of Bishops by Pope Clement VIII., in 1600, simply confirmed a custom which had already become almost universal.

It is however worthy of note that the Ceremonial of Bishops, while prescribing purple as the proper color for the Bishop's dress, did not abolish the established tradition of using *green* as the distinctive episcopal color; nay, it confirmed it by ordaining that *green* should be the color of the principal token of the episcopal dignity the pontifical hat. Roman usage, in accordance with this accepted tradition, and the known mind of the compilers of the *Caeremoniale Episcoporum,* has always emphasized the principle that green is the episcopal color, except for the Bishop's clothes; for instance, green is the habitual color of the drapery on the Bishop's throne and prie-dieu, of the canopy over his coat-of-arms in the hall of his house, of the plumes on the harness of his horses, when he rides in state, and of the cushion which, before 1870, was carried by a valet for the Bishop to kneel on in the not unfrequent case when he would meet on the streets of Rome a priest carrying the blessed Sacrament to the sick.

Purple is substituted for green in several of these articles during penitential seasons, like Advent, Septuagesima and fast days, as also when the Holy See is vacant and at funerals. On these occasions, the draperies of the Bishop's throne and kneeler should be purple, in sign of penitence and mourning. On festival days, however, when the Bishop officiates from the throne, the draperies should be of the color prescribed by the rubrics for the sacred vestments.

If the Prelate is a Cardinal, purple is used on the same occasions as for a Bishop; but scarlet red is invariably used whenever green is prescribed by episcopal etiquette.

As a practical conclusion of the foregoing principles, one sees that whenever a celebration is held in honor of an Archbishop or Bishop, the color to be used for the decorations of the house, church, hall or street, the ribbons or strings which adorn or bind the programs, menu-cards, engraved addresses, and the like, should not be purple, but *green.*

2. There is another tradition or rule which is sometimes lost sight of, it is that of *harmony* in the prelatial dress, a rule called in some liturgical books "the law of equilibrium", the violations of which are permissible only to Prelates whose financial resources are insufficient, which is not generally the case in this country. According to this rule, the main parts of a Prelate's costume should match one another in material as well as in color. For instance, a Bishop should not wear a purple *mozzetta* over a black cassock; a Cardinal

should not wear a red silk *mozzetta* over a winter cassock of red cloth; a Domestic Prelate should not put on a woolen *mantelletta* over a silk cassock, etc., etc. The only exception to this general rule is in the *cappa magna* of Bishops - the Bishop's *cappa magna* is always purple, whatever be the color of his cassock. Prelates should also take care that the hue of the purple be the same in the mozzetta or mantelletta as in the cassock.

3. The costume of Cardinals, Archbishops and Bishops attending a funeral service is, according to the Ceremonial, the penitential dress; therefore a Cardinal should vest in purple, trimmed in scarlet, while Archbishops and Bishops should wear the black cassock and the mantelletta (or mozzetta, as the case may be) of the same color, all the parts of this choir dress being lined and trimmed in purple. Only the Prelates *di mantelletta* and *di mantellone* should wear purple at a funeral service, because they do not put on mourning, except on the death of the Sovereign Pontiff and on Good Friday.

The practice in Rome, which has several times been objected to the present writer as condemning this principle, is indeed different, inasmuch as the Bishops who attend a Requiem in Rome are directed to dress in purple; but the reason for that difference is that the etiquette of the Roman court forbids at all times in Rome the wearing of mourning by Bishops, except on Good Friday and during the vacancy of the Holy See; in other words, the Bishops in Rome follow the same rule as is observed every where by the Domestic Prelates and the Prelates *di mantellone*.

Connected with this, is the rule concerning the preaching of a funeral eulogy. All know that the Prelate or priest who delivers such an oration does not put on his choir habit. But the cassock does not by itself constitute a complete ecclesiastical dress, and a Prelate or a priest should never appear before the public without being completely and correctly dressed. Now, as, in this case, the orator, though speaking in church, is not authorized to vest in his rochet or surplice, he should throw on his shoulders the ecclesiastical cloak (*ferraiolo* or *ferraiolone*), which completes the clerical costume in default of the choir insignia. Therefore, if the orator is a priest, he should wear a black cassock and a black cloak of woolen material; if an Archbishop or Bishop, a black cassock, or simar, trimmed with purple, a black cincture and a black silk cloak. Should it happen that a Cardinal delivers such a sermon a rather rare occurrence his cassock should be black with red trimmings; his cincture, purple; and his cloak, purple, with scarlet trimmings; but, for the reason above given, Domestic Prelates do not wear the prelatial mourning dress on that occasion, except when the funeral oration is in honor of a deceased Sovereign Pontiff.

In some parts of the country, owing to the influence of Bishops and priests who have sojourned or studied in Rome, the wearing of the Roman cloak becomes more aid more frequent. Such tendency is most correct and deserves encouragement. Clergy men should know that the cloak is the necessary complement of the ecclesiastical dress outside church ceremonies, and has, besides, the advantage of being very elegant. Prelates and priests would do well to take the habit of wearing it, whenever it is possible for them to do so. Some occasions, on which it is proper for ecclesiastics to wear the cloak were mentioned in the chapter of this book, where the rules concerning the making up and wearing of this garment are especially dealt with, and others will be detailed in the following chapter.

It now remains to study the different costumes which each class of Prelates is privileged, as well as bound, to wear.

Costumes of a Cardinal

4. A Cardinal wears, according to circumstances, the church dress, the etiquette dress known as *abito piano,* or the academic dress.

The church dress is of two sorts, one for solemnities the other for less formal occasions.

The solemn church dress consists of the choir cassock, the cincture with gold tassels, the rochet with scarlet lining, the cappa magna, the skull-cap and the biretta. With this costume, the Cardinal wears scarlet stockings and shoes of red morocco leather with gold buckles; but he does not wear gloves; neither should the pectoral cross appear, or, if it is used at all, it should be worn under the cappa magna, and the proper ring to be worn with this costume is the cardinalitial ring adorned with a sapphire.

A Cardinal in Solemn Church Dress

Independently of the season, the cincture and the cappa magna, as well as the skull-cap, always are of scarlet red watered silk; but the material of the cassock and of the biretta changes with the season, scarlet watered silk is used in summer, and fine red broadcloth in winter.

On penitential days and occasions of mourning, the color of the Cardinal's solemn church dress is somewhat modified; the cassock, cincture and cappa magna are purple instead of red, but the other portions of the costume remain unchanged. On Good Friday, in sign of deep mourning, Cardinals wear a cappa magna of purple serge; this being the only day in the year when they do not wear a watered silk cappa magna.

The other church dress of a Cardinal is less solemn: in his titular church in Rome, and every where outside of Rome, this costume consists of the choir cassock, the cincture with gold tassels, the rochet with scarlet lining, the mozzetta, the skull cap, the biretta and the cardinalitial ring adorned with a sapphire; the stockings are scarlet, and the shoes may be either of red morocco or of black patent leather with red heels. Over the mozzetta, the Cardinal wears the pontifical pectoral cross suspended from a gold cord, fitted at the neck with the slide, and the tassel hanging over the back; the ordinary pectoral cross with a chain instead of a cord is indeed tolerated, but it is less formal, and the Roman masters of ceremonies do not readily allow its use.

In Rome, outside of his titular church, a Cardinal adds to this costume the mantelletta which he wears under the mozzetta. The cassock, the mantelletta, the mozzetta and the biretta are of scarlet watered silk in summer and of fine broadcloth in winter; but the cincture and the skull-cap are of watered silk at all times.

On penitential days and times of mourning, this costume is modified as to the color; the cassock, the cincture, the mantelletta and the mozzetta are then purple instead of scarlet.

On other occasions, a Cardinal wears the "eti-

Simple Church Dress of a Cardinal in Rome

quette dress usually called by liturgists *abito piano,* because it was decreed by Pope Pius IX. This costume consists of the black cassock or simar trimmed in scarlet, the red cincture with fringes, the red cloak (*ferraiolone*), the red skull-cap and, according to circumstances, the red biretta or the black hat with a red and gold cord or band and tassels. The stockings are of red silk, and the shoes of black patent leather with red heels and gold buckles. If the Cardinal wears the hat, he should also have gloves of red silk; the wearing of the biretta makes this costume semi-informal and excludes the wearing of gloves. This costume is completed by the ordinary pectoral cross, hanging from a gold chain, worn over the cassock or simar, under the cloak, and by the cardinalitial ring which must remain apparent even when the Prelate wears gloves.

On penitential and mourning occasions, the cincture should be purple instead of red; the cloak (*ferraiolone*) also is purple, but with red lining and trimmings; the other parts of the costume remain the same as at ordinary times.

This costume remains practically unchanged throughout the year, the only difference being that, in summer, the cassock or simar is made of lighter material. If the temperature is too cold for wearing the *ferraiolone,* the Cardinal may wear the large cloak of broadcloth, red at ordinary times, purple, on penitential days, or even black if the occasion is quite informal.

The third costume of a Cardinal is a formal court dress which is known among liturgists as the "academic dress" from the fact that it is used by Cardinals when attending solemn academic functions in Rome. It consists of the scarlet cassock, the cincture with gold tassels, the mozzetta, the pectoral cross suspended from its gold chain, and the red cloak (*ferraiolone*), the small hood of the mozzetta being thrown back over the collar of the cloak. With this costume, the Cardinal should wear gloves of red silk, with the cardinalitial ring over the gloved fourth finger of the right hand, low shoes of red morocco leather, with gold buckles, and the ordinary hat of red felt, with a cord or band and tassels of red silk entwined with gold.

Costumes of an Archbishop or Bishop within his Jurisdiction

5. The costumes of an Archbishop or Bishop indicative of his jurisdiction are the "church dress" and the "academic dress".

The "church dress" is of two sorts:- the solemn and the informal.

The solemn church dress consists of the choir cassock with the cincture ending in tufts, the rochet, the cappa magna, the skull-cap and the biretta. These articles are of the regular purple color with crimson lining; the cassock and the cappa magna of woolen material, and the other pieces of the cost ume of plain silk; the linen rochet is lined at the cuffs with red silk. The stockings are of purple silk, and the shoes, of patent leather with gold buckles. With this costume, the Prelate wears the episcopal ring, but the pectoral cross should not appear if worn at all, it should be worn under the cappa magna. Formerly, the Prelate wore also the green pontifical hat; but the use of that head-dress has nowadays become obsolete; however, the Prellate may have it carried behind him by an attendant.

At funeral ceremonies and on penitential days, or during the vacancy of the Holy See, this costume consists of the same articles as above; but the cassock is the mourning choir cassock, black with purple trimmings, the cincture is of black silk and the rochet cuffs are lined in purple.

The informal church dress comprises the choir cassock, the cincture with tufts, the rochet, the mozetta, the skull-cap and the biretta; it is completed with purple silk stockings, shoes of patent leather with gold buckles, the episcopal ring and the pectoral cross. When possible, the pectoral cross should be the "pontifical cross" suspended from a green and gold cord.

On ordinary occasions, the various parts of this costume are purple, and the rochet cuffs are lined with red silk; but, for mourning and penitential wear, the cassock and the mozetta are black with purple lining and trimmings, the cuffs of the rochet are lined with purple silk and the cincture is wholly black; the color of the other articles does not change.

The presence of a Cardinal restricts the display of the signs of jurisdiction by the Ordinary, unless he be a Cardinal himself. Therefore, in presence of a Cardinal, the only church dress allowed an Archbishop or a Bishop within his jurisdiction consists of the choir cassock, cincture, rochet, mantelletta and mozetta; the other articles being as described for the informal church dress. If the Cardinal has the title of Legate *a latere,* every sign of jurisdiction should disappear from the costume of the Ordinary who then should wear the costume prescribed for a Bishop outside his territory; an Archbishop or a Bishop is never allowed to wear the mozetta in presence of a Papal Legate.

The "academic dress" or "court dress", to be worn at solemn academic functions and official audiences of a Sovereign, consists of the purple choir cassock, cincture with tufts, mozetta and ferraiolone, with the hood of the mozetta thrown over the collar of the ferraiolone. To complete this costume, the Prelate wears the skull-cap and the black hat with green band (or cord) and tassels, purple silk stockings and patent leather shoes with gold buckles. The pectoral cross to be used is the "episcopal cross" hanging from its gold chain, which is worn over the mozetta. With this costume, the Prelate is expected to wear purple silk gloves, with the episcopal ring over the gloved finger. Before being admitted to the official audience of a sovereign Prince or President of a Republic, the Prelate should however remove his gloves, for court etiquette usually forbids the wearing of gloves by civilians in presence of the head of a sovereign State.

Costumes of an Archbishop or Bishop outside his Jurisdiction

6. Outside his jurisdiction, an Archbishop or Bishop has not the right to wear the cappa magna or the mozetta. His church dress comprises the choir cassock, the cincture with tufts, the rochet and the mantelletta. He wears the skull-cap and the biretta, purple silk stockings and patent leather shoes with gold buckles. At funerals and on penitential days, as well as during the vacancy of the Holy See, the cassock and the mantelletta are black, lined and trimmed in purple, and the cincture is entirely black; but, at other times these articles are of the usual purple color. The lining of the rochet cuffs changes

also as was indicated above. With this costume, the Prelate wears the pectoral cross suspended from a green and gold chain or, by mere toleration, from a gold chain.

The "academic dress or "court dress" of an Archbishop or Bishop outside his jurisdiction consists of the choir cassock, the cincture with tufts, the mantelletta, silk stockings, skull-cap and gloves, all these articles in purple; his shoes are of patent leather with gold buckles; he wears the pectoral cross hanging from a gold chain, the ordinary episcopal ring over the gloved finger, and the black hat with a green band (or cord) and tassels. What was said above concerning the removal of gloves in presence of a Sovereign applies also in this case.

Costume of Archbishops and Bishops Independently of the Jurisdiction

7. The only official costume common to all Archbishops and Bishops independently of their jurisdiction is the informal court dress known as *abito piano*.

The *abito piano* or, as it is sometimes called, the "etiquette dress" consists of the black cassock or simar trimmed in amaranth red, the purple cincture with fringes, the cloak (*ferraiolone*), the skull-cap and the black hat with a green band (or cord) and tassels, the gloves and stockings are of purple silk and the shoes of patent leather with gold buckles The Prelate wears the pectoral cross suspended from its gold chain and the episcopal ring. As was said above, in the description of a Cardinal's *abito piano*, the biretta may, for semi-informal wear, be used instead of the hat; but, in this case, the Prelate should not wear gloves.

On occasions of mourning on penitential days and during the vacancy of the Holy See, the *abito piano* of Archbishops and Bishops varies in color according to already stated principles: the cassock or simar is black with purple lining and trimmings, the cincture and the ferraiolone are entirely black; but the other parts of the costume retain their usual colors.

On all occasions, when the temperature is too cold for the use of the ferraiolone, the winter cloak of broadcloth may be substituted: the cloak is purple in color at ordinary times and black for penitential or mourning occasions. For less formal dress, the cloak may be black at all times; but, whatever its color, the cloak is fastened in front with a silver clasp, and an Archbishop's cloak is differenced from a Bishop's by a border of gold braid around the bottom of the cape.

Costumes of Domestic Prelates

8. The three official costumes of a Domestic Prelate are the "church dress", the "*abito piano*" and the "academic dress".

The church dress comprises the purple choir cassock, the purple cincture with tufts, the rochet with red lining, the purple mantelletta, the black skull-cap trimmed in amaranth red, the black biretta with a purple tuft (a red tuft for a Protonotary Apostolic), purple silk stockings and patent leather shoes with gold buckles. If the Prelate is entitled to wear a ring, he may do so within the limits of the indult of concession. A Protonotary Apostolic *ad instar participantium* may also wear the pectoral cross hanging from a purple silk cord over the mantelletta, but only before and after his Pontifical Mass.

During the vacancy of the Holy See and on Good Friday, Domestic Prelates wear the penitential church dress consisting of the black choir cassock trimmed and lined in purple, the black cincture, the rochet with purple lining, the black mantelletta lined and trimmed in purple, and the other parts of the costume as described in the preceding paragraph.

The *abito piano* of a Domestic Prelate is similar to a Bishop s, with the exception of the hat which is adorned with a purple band (or cord) and tassels (the cord and tassels being red for a Protonotary Apostolic). If the biretta is used instead of the more formal hat, it must be the regular biretta granted Domestic Prelates by the brief *Inter multiplices,* that is a black biretta with no other ornament than a purple tuft (a red tuft for a Protonotary Apostolic). Needless to say, the Prelate dues not wear the pectoral cross; but he may wear a ring if he is enlidedto that distinction.

The "academic dress" or "court dress" of a Domestic Prelate is nearly the same as is prescribed for a Bishop outside his jurisdiction. The cassock and the manteletta are of plain silk in summer and of fine broadcloth in winter; the hat is ornamented with a purple band (or cord) and tassels (red for a Protonotary Apostolic), and the Prelate does not wear the pectoral cross, but he may wear a ring, if he is entitled to do so by law or privilege.

Costumes of a Prelate *di Mantellone.*

9. The Pope's Chamberlains and Chaplains (Prelates *di mantellone*) have, like the Domestic Prelates, a "church dress" and an "*abito piano.*"

The church dress consists of the purple cassock without a train, the purple cincture with tufts, the purple mantellone, the black skull cap and the black biretta. They do not wear the rochet. The stockings are of purple silk (black in Rome), and the shoes of patent leather with gold buckles.

This costume serves also the purpose of an academic dress"; but the black hat with purple (black in Rome) band (or cord) and tassels is then worn instead of the biretta, and the Prelate wears purple silk gloves (black in Rome).

The *abito piano* or "etiquette dress" of a Prelate *di mantellone* consists of the black cassock or simar trimmed in purple, the ferraiolone of black silk, the black skull-cap and the black hat with purple (black in Rome) band (or cord) and tassels. The stockings and gloves are of purple silk outside of Rome, but black in Rome; the shoes are of patent leather with gold buckles.

The winter cloak, if used, is always black, and may be fastened with a silver clasp.

If a Chamberlain or Chaplain to His Holiness is called upon to perform his functions at the Vatican, he wears, on certain solemn occasions, the red crocia instead of the purple mantellone; but it must be remembered that the crocia, which was described at the end of the chapter on the mantellone, is not worn outside the Roman curia, except when a Papal Chamberlain is despatched as special messenger (*ablegate*) of the Sovereign Pontiff to deliver the red biretta to a newly appointed Cardinal.

Chapter Nine - Costumes to be Worn by Prelates on Different Occasions

1. Whenever a Prelate appears in his official capacity, his duty is to wear the costume suited to the occasion. The law of the Church, expressed in many decrees of the Sacred Congregations, makes this principle imperative, and the wishes of our Catholic people are fully in accordance with it; nothing makes our people so wholesomely proud of their religion as to witness a public church ceremony in which their Prelates take part, and they feel a thrill of loyalty when a crowd of non-Catholic onlookers bend over the ropes to obtain a good view of a solemn procession graced and made color ful by the presence of many Prelates. The time is now passed when a good-natured disregard for the formalities of ceremonial was accepted by many as a sign of broad-mindedness and loyal Americanism". Too long have some priests and Prelates seemed to regard a display of accurate ceremonial and etiquette as savoring of "Old World traditions"; the much misunderstood and misquoted "Jeffersonian simplicity" belongs to an age that is past, and allusions to it are nowadays permissible only to political orators. Now, as in all ages, the human eye is fond of color, and we have in the ceremonial of the Catholic Church a treasure which is envied by the outsiders and has been entrusted to us that we may open it to all and spend it lavishly.

It is an admitted fact, plain to every man who has had the opportunity and the taste to observe the manifestations of public sentiment, that the American people is fond of ceremonial display. Travelling agencies advertise famous ceremonies abroad, and yearly reap a rich harvest of American dollars from the throngs of tourists attracted to foreign lands by the desire of witnessing those *Catholic* ceremonies. But we have at home, in our most modest cathedrals, the means of attracting a proportionate crowd of interested admirers. The ceremonies of our Church are no longer despised and condemned by our non-Catholic brethren, and we should make no sacrifice of our ritual to their supposed prejudices, for those prejudices no longer exist in the mass; not a genuflection, not a bow, not a single article of costume, should be omitted under the fallacious pretext that "it would shock the

Protestants". It will not shock them; the few who might still be "shocked" do not attend our services, and the great majority of others expect, on the contrary, to see the exact performance of our ceremonies, and would indeed be "shocked" if they knew that some elements have been omitted on account of so-called prejudices which seldom, if ever, enter their minds.

We may therefore state as a principle that there is nothing in the actual spirit or customs of this country that may hinder the full display of prelatial ceremonial. Nor are we in any way impeded by "immemorial customs" of our own, for the decrees of the Plenary Councils of Baltimore banish foreign liturgical practices, and direct that our ceremonial is, and must remain, exclusively Roman. Finally, an untrammeled performance of our ceremonial in all its details is, in itself, a public, if silent, assertion that the Catholic Church is determined to avail herself of the freedom of religious worship guaranteed to every citizen in this Republic, as it is also a public denial of the maxim, so much exploited abroad by non-Catholic missionaries, that "America is a Protestant country".

It is in the light of the foregoing principles that one should read the following regulations laid down by the Roman ceremonial as to the costumes which the several classes of Prelates must wear on different occasions.

2. From the day on which he has received the official notification of his elevation to the episcopate, a Bishop may wear all the insignia of his new dignity, except those which are to be conferred during the ceremony of his episcopal consecration. Therefore a Bishop-Elect dresses on all occasions like a consecrated Bishop, except that he does not wear the pectoral cross and the ring.

On the morning of his consecration, the Elect takes part in the preliminary procession, wearing the "church dress", as described in the preceding chapter (except the pectoral cross and the ring), all purple, including the skull-cap and the biretta. [1] The church dress prescribed is the solemn, and therefore includes the cappa magna, if the Elect is consecrated in the diocese which he has been appointed to govern; otherwise, the "church dress" is that of a Bishop outside his jurisdiction. If the consecration took place in presence of a Cardinal, the new Bishop, consecrated in his own diocese, should abstain from wearing the cappa magna, and should wear instead the mantelletta and the mozzetta; the mozzetta itself being put aside if the Cardinal had the title of Legate *a latere*.

The present writer has frequently been asked by diocesan masters of ceremonies where they could find directions for the ceremony of a Bishop's "installation". In every case, he was forced to answer that there exists no such ceremony. The so-called "installation" is a pure "Americanism", a relic of our missionary period. In the course of the nineteenth century, when new dioceses were frequently created in consequence of the rapid growth of the Catholic population, it may have at times appeared necessary to the Bishop whose diocese had just been dismembered to present to the people of the new diocese the Prelate to whom they were henceforth to give their allegiance; but our Church has now attained considerable stability, and the limits of dioceses seldom change; moreover the press informs the people of the death, resignation or translation of their Ordinary, announces the appointment of the new Bishop, describes his person and his career, and publishes his portrait; the presentation, which, in olden times, might have been necessary, is now useless. On the other hand, the new Ordinary should, according to the letter and the spirit of the Ceremonial, appear to his people for the first time in full possession of his authority: nobody is qualified to present him to his people and lead him to his throne; to do so would signify an assumption of authority which the Sovereign Pontiff alone could claim *de potentia absoluta*, but never exercises in fact.

The Ceremonial of Bishops (Book I., Ch. II.) describes the ceremony of the Bishop's solemn entry into his episcopal city, and the directions therein given should be followed accurately, excepting of course the details which have become obsolete, as, for instance, the cavalcade; the caparisoned horse of the seventeenth century having been, in later times, replaced by an open carriage, and, more recently, by a motor car. For that ceremony, the Ordinary, before vesting in the Pontifical vestments as prescribed by the rubrics, should wear the "solemn church dress" of purple, and it would therefore be contrary to the meaning of the ceremony to invite a higher Prelate whose presence would force the Ordinary to abstain from wearing the costume significant of his jurisdiction. [2]

The "solemn church dress" is also required whenever an Ordinary attends a ceremony of some importance within the territory submitted to his jurisdiction, such as solemn mass, vespers or other solemn service, ordinations, consecrations, laying of a corner stone, processions, etc. It is especially prescribed for attendance at the services on the last three days of Holy Week. The office of Matins, commonly known as *Tenebrae*, is not an exception; it is a solemn service (*duplex primes classis*), and the Bishop is directed to attend it vested in cappa magna, with the restriction however that he is not allowed the services of a train-bearer when moving from the altar of the Blessed Sacrament to the throne. (*Caer. Episc.* Lib. II., Cap. XXII.)

Whatever is said here of the "solemn church dress" to be worn by an Archbishop or Bishop within his territory applies to a Cardinal every where outside of Rome. In Rome, the wearing of the "solemn church dress" by a Cardinal is determined by the Sacred Congregation of the Ceremonial, and Cardinals taking part in any important function receive for their guidance printed directions from the Pontifical Masters of Ceremonies. In default of such instructions, a Cardinal attending a function in Rome, may confidently rely on the experience of the competent train-bearer who is assigned to him during his sojourn in the Papal City.

Strictly speaking, an Archbishop or a Bishop should not sit upon his throne, unless vested in the cappa magna; of late, however, the Sacred Congregation of Rites has allowed more liberty, chiefly in favor of missionary Bishops prevented by the modicity of their resources from owning a cappa magna, as also in order to obviate the difficulty of finding a suitable place for the Ordinary in the sanctuary of chapels or small churches; but a Bishop who can afford to own a cappa magna should not avail himself of that tolerance when attending a service in his cathedral.

Our Bishops have, in this country, the laudable - and by their clergy much appreciated - custom of attending in person the funerals of their priests. There is of course no special prescription as to the kind of church dress to be worn by the Ordinary on such an occasion; but it seems that the funeral of a priest who has exercised the sacred ministry and endeared himself to his people could well be regarded as a solemn function, and the presence of the Ordinary vested in cappa magna would singularly enhance the solemnity of the occasion.

Cardinals, Archbishops and Bishops, attending a funeral service, should wear the mourning, or penitential, church dress; but Domestic Prelates and Prelates *di mantellone* have not that privilege; they alone should wear the purple church dress at funeral services, as has been mentioned before. Domestic Prelates, however, should appear in mourning church dress at a Requiem celebrated for the repose of the soul of the Sovereign Pontiff; and, on the same occasion, Prelates *di mantellone,* who have no official mourning church dress, should wear a black cassock and a surplice.

At the public sessions of a Plenary or Provincial Council, Archbishops and Bishops attend vested in cope and mitre; but, at the other sessions, they should wear the "informal church dress" of an Ordinary within his territory - the cassock, the cincture, the rochet and the mozzetta - because they then exercise jurisdiction in a body, *per modum unius.*

The other occasions on which an Archbishop or a Bishop wears the "informal church dress" within the limits of his jurisdiction are many and various; liturgists mention, the examination of candidates for "approbation" or for religious profession; spiritual exercises; pastoral retreat; familiar instructions; attendance at services without solemnity, in which case the Ordinary should, strictly speaking, occupy the first stall in the choir; pastoral visitations or inspections; administering the oath and profession of faith to newly appointed clergymen; and other acts of spiritual ministration not requiring solemnity. When the Ordinary wears the informal church dress, he is not entitled to the assistance of two priests.

Archbishops and Bishops outside of their respective territories, Domestic Prelates and Prelates *di mantellone,* when attending church ceremonies, should wear the "church dress" as described in the preceding chapter, according to their several degrees in the Prelature.

With regard to the administration of the sacraments or sacramentals, which requires the wearing of a stole, all Prelates and Canons privileged to wear a cape of any form (mozzetta, cappa, mantelletta or mantellone) must remember that the Sovereign Pontiff is the only Prelate who may wear a stole over his cape. Therefore, a Prelate about to administer a sacrament or a sacramental, for which he is directed to wear a stole, must first remove his cape; then, if he be a Cardinal, an Archbishop or a Bishop, he puts on the stole over the rochet; if he be a Domestic Prelate or a Canon entitled to wear the rochet, he puts on a surplice (or *cotta*) over the rochet, and the stole over the surplice (or *cotta*); if he be a Chamberlain or Chaplain to His Holiness, he simply puts on a surplice (or *cotta*) over the cassock, and a stole over the surplice (or *cotta*). The prohibition to wear the stole over a cape applies also, *et a fortiori,* to all other liturgical vestments, the cope being here particularly meant. When a Domestic Prelate (or a Canon having the privilege of wearing the rochet) is to wear a cope, he must first remove his cape and put on an amice over the rochet.

The number of Roman Prelates having greatly increased of late years, it not infrequently happens that Domestic Prelates or Prelates *di mantellone* are designated to serve as "Chaplains" or "Assistants" to the Bishop during a procession, mass or other ceremony. These "Assistants" or "Chaplains" are often incorrectly referred to as "Deacons of Honor". There is first to be made an important distinction, in order to prevent the spread of an abuse coming from a too general ignorance of the real status of Roman Prelates. The "Deacons of Honor" are not any kind of clerics appointed to sit with the Bishop, walk by his sides and assist him at low Mass; they are the two clergy men (Canons, when the cathedral is regularly constituted) who dress in Deacons vestments to assist the Bishop at Pontifical Mass or Vespers: at the beginning of the ceremony, they step aside or go to the sacristy, and put on the diaconal vestments. The two priests who escort the Bishop at processions, sit alongside of him when he wears the cappa magna, or serve him at low Mass, are not "Deacons of Honor", but "Assistants", or, as they are frequently, but less correctly, called, "Chaplains".

From this it follows that a Domestic Prelate or a Chamberlain may well act as "Deacon of Honor", for, in that office, his Prelacy is not apparent, since he is vested as a Deacon; but it is an error to designate Prelates to act as "Assistants" to a Bishop, for they have been made Prelates for the exclusive service of His Holiness, and no Cardinal or Bishop has a right to their personal service in their capacity as Prelates; it is an abasement of their dignity to make them appear publicly in their prelatial dress as ministers to a Cardinal or a Bishop.

The same remarks apply to the officer who is commonly known as "Assistant Priest" (often, but very incorrectly, as "Archpriest"). When a Bishop celebrates Pontifical Mass or Vespers, a Domestic Prelate or Chamberlain may act as "Assistant Priest", for he then wears the cope, and his prelatial dress does not appear; but the priest who simply escorts the Bishop and sits near him in choir habit must not be taken from the ranks of the Roman Prelature.

If it were impossible to find other clergymen to assist the Bishop an evidently rare occurrence , Roman Prelates could be designated for that office; but, in that case, they should take off the mantelletta or mantellone, and put on a surplice the Domestic Prelates, over the rochet; and the Chamberlains, over the cassock.

3. On formal occasions other than church ceremonies or religious ministrations, Prelates wear the *abito piano* and the "academic dress".

The *abito piano* is prescribed for receptions of all sorts, audiences to delegations, banquets, entertainments in schools and academies, and whenever a Prelate is expected to appear in public in his official capacity in circumstances and places which allow him to wear the cassock.

It is also the proper dress for official calls which a Prelate owes to other Prelates or lay dignitaries in Rome or in countries where local custom and usage permits the full ecclesiastical dress in civil life, such as Italy, France, Spain, Belgium, in the countries of South East Europe and in Asia. In those countries, Prelates usually wear the *abito piano* in all circumstances for which social customs and etiquette require the formal dress for a lay gentleman, namely, visits, receptions, dinners, concerts, etc. In America, the abito piano is seldom required in mere social life; but it is decidedly gaining popular ity in society circles, and some distinguished hostesses are now evidently grateful to an invited Prelate in he appears, at the dinner hour, as Cardinal Gibbons was wont to do in the last years of his life, in the official dress which he would wear in similar circumstances in Italy or in France.

Since 1870, the *abito piano* is the required costume for papal audiences. Before that time, Bishops and Prelates admitted to the presence of the Sovereign Pontiff wore the purple church dress ". Pope Pius IX. having ordered that change of etiquette to institute a marked difference in the ceremonial of his court after the loss of his temporal power, the new style of court dress was henceforth called *abito piano*. Prelates received by the Sovereign Pontiff are relieved of their hats by the *Bussolanti,* and they must remove their gloves before entering the Pope's apartment. The only persons allowed to wear gloves in the Pope's presence are royal princesses and men in military or naval uniform; foreign ambassadors and ministers accredited to the Vatican have the privilege of appearing before the Pope holding the right glove in the gloved left hand.

The "academic dress", as its name indicates, is chiefly worn at academic solemnities. Etiquette prescribes it in Rome for public sessions of the pontifical academies, and it may be used at home for important scholastic events in Catholic Colleges and Universities, such as the solemn opening of the academic term, graduation exercises, foundation of a chair, inauguration of a new Rector, and other extraordinary circumstances. For academic events of minor importance, such as occur in parochial or high schools, academies and small colleges, a Prelate may appropriately wear the *abito piano*.

The "academic dress" is at the same time a solemn "court dress", and is the proper costume to be worn by a Prelate admitted, in his prelatial capacity or as representative of the Sovereign Pontiff, to the official audience of a reigning Prince or President of a Republic; but local customs and court regulations sometimes modify this point of etiquette; so that a Prelate, before such an audience, would do well to inquire from authorized persons what is the precise local usage, and follow it accurately.

4. Most cases are covered by the rules given in the preceding pages; but it is evidently impossible to foresee all occasions or circumstances when a Prelate is expected to wear a definite costume; hence our Prelates are allowed a great deal of liberty to choose their costumes for the different circumstances according to local usage and their personal comfort and convenience; the general rule being always to keep as close as possible to the prescriptions of the Roman ceremonial, and not to make an incongruous mixture of ecclesiastical and civil garments.

5. This chapter will be concluded with a few remarks concerning the laying out of the remains of a deceased Prelate.

The law of the Church is that a dead ecclesiastic should be laid out vested in the insignia of the office or dignity which he held while living; but this principle must be rightly understood.

As the priestly or episcopal character is what is the most important in the person of an ecclesiastic, and, according to the teaching of the Church, is destined to last forever, the law is that the body of a dead priest or Bishop should be dressed in his sacerdotal or episcopal vestments. There are indeed exceptions, but, in this case, they can be said to confirm the rule. By sacerdotal or episcopal vestments, we mean such ornaments as the Prelate or priest should put on while preparing for the celebration of solemn High Mass, which is the greatest act that a Prelate or priest can perform.

These vestments should be of purple color. [3] Therefore, the body of a deceased priest will be vested in his ordinary cassock; amice, alb, cingulum, purple maniple, stole and chasuble; shoes will be put on his feet, and the biretta on his head. A prevailing abuse consists in placing a naked chalice between the clasped hands of the deceased; this is indeed a touching symbol, but such practice should not be retained; the chalice being necessarily placed perpendicular to the body, such a disposition looks very awkward and unnatural; and, moreover, it is opposed to the spirit of the Church to expose sacred vessels - especially the chalice - to the public gaze; finally, the Church directs that a crucifix should be placed between the hands of the deceased ecclesiastic.

When a Cardinal dies in Rome, his body is laid out vested in the choir dress which Cardinals usually wear while in Rome; but, if the Cardinal is, at the same time, a residential Bishop and dies outside of Rome, the regulations to be followed in laying out his remains are the same as for an ordinary Bishop.

When the Bishop has breathed his last and his body has been properly embalmed, his attendants vest him in his mourning choir cassock - black trimmed in purple, for an Archbishop or a Bishop; purple, trimmed in scarlet, for a Cardinal. The train of the cassock should not be unfolded, for this is re-garded as a sign of jurisdiction, and all jurisdiction ceases at the death of the Prelate. Over the cassock, they put the cincture - black for a Bishop, purple for a Cardinal - and the rochet. They then vest the Prelate in his pontificals of purple - stockings and sandals, amice, alb, cingulum, pectoral cross without relics, stole, tunic and dalmatic, gloves, chasuble and maniple. On the fourth finger of the right hand they put the ring, clasp his hands on his breast and place between them a crucifix, tying them with a purple silk ribbon to hold them in place, if necessary.

If the Prelate was a Metropolitan - or otherwise entitled to wear the palli-um - they place the pallium over his shoulders, if he is laid out within the lim-its of his territorial jurisdiction; if outside, the pallium should be placed un-der his head. If he has been the incumbent of several archbishoprics, the pal-liums of his previous sees should also be placed under his head.

The crosier, as being the main sign of jurisdiction, should not be placed in the dead Prelate's hands, or alongside of his body, or even in the room where the remains are laid out.

On his head, the attendants place the skull-cap - red or purple - and the simple mitre of white silk. At the foot of the bier they hang the pontifical hat, red for a Cardinal, green for an Archbishop or a Bishop.

The room where the body of the Prelate is laid out should be furnished with chairs or benches, so as to accommodate the clergy, who ought to recite there the "Office of the Dead."

A crucifix, between two lighted candles, is placed on a credence-table, with a black stole and a black cope, the holy-water vessel, the censer and the in-cense-boat.

It would be proper also to erect a temporary altar, so as to have Masses celebrated in the room. Requiem Masses *"in die obitus episcopi"* [4] may be celebrated there for the deceased Prelate, as long as the body remains ex-posed, except if the day is a "double of first class," or excluding the celebrat ion of a feast of first class.

The clergy recite the Office of the Dead, and, at the end of each Nocturn, of Lauds, and of Vespers, the senior member of the clergy puts on the stole and the cope and gives the absolution.

The coffin should be lined in purple, and, on its lid, a metallic plate should bear engraved the name and coat-or-arms of the Prelate, with the date of his death.

The practice, which is in vogue in some parts of the country, to veil or drape in black the throne of the departed Bishop, should be abandoned. The throne should be hung in purple and used by the presiding Prelate, if this is a Cardi-nal or the Metropolitan of the deceased Bishop. The practice of veiling the throne and leaving it unoccupied is an old French importation, and, as such, opposed by decrees of the plenary councils of Baltimore, which prohibit any foreign customs from being introduced into the liturgy of this country. [5]

The remains of Prelates inferior to Bishops are laid out vested in the purple cassock and priestly vestments. If the dead Prelate had the privilege of the pontificals - as is the case for Protonotaries Apostolic - he may be vested in his pontificals; but the mitre should not be put on his head; his proper head-dress is the prelatial biretta.

After the burial of a Cardinal, or of a Bishop, his pontifical hat is suspended to the ceiling of the church, above the place where the body is interred.

[1] Among several unpleasant recollections in this matter, the writer remembers the peremptory rebuke administered to him by a well-meaning Archbishop for modestly presuming to inform a Bishop-Elect about to be consecrated that the proper head-dress for the occasion was the purple biretta.
[2] One can readily see the contradiction between the spirit of that ceremony and its actual performance, if the new Bishop were "installed" by a Cardinal, in which case, the Ordinary would for the first time appear before his people in a humiliated condition, as he should abase his jurisdiction before the Cardinal's dignity, by abstaining from the use of the cappa magna, covering his rochet with the mantelletta, and yielding his throne to the Cardinal.
[3] The Sacred Congregation of Rites now tolerates the use of black vestments; but purple remains preferable, and should be used when ever possible.
[4] That Mass is the first Mass of All Souls Day, with the special orations for a deceased Prelate.
[5] *Concil. Plen. Baltim.* I., nn. 36, 42, 44. – *Concil. Plen. Baltim.* II., nn. 210, 213, 216, 218.

Chapter Ten - Privileges of Doctors

1. The Doctorate (from *docere,* to teach) is an academic distinction giving the right of publicly teaching the subject in which one has obtained this degree.

However, if the doctorate confers a *right,* it does not confer a *mission,* and, as is well explained in the diplomas delivered by the Roman universities, a doctor can not teach without having been positively appointed by his Ordinary.

The doctorate creates a *de jure* presumption in favor of the candidate for teaching, so that his Bishop can not legally require from him an examination before appointing him to a chair. But, this presumption exists only when it is question of teaching; a doctor as such is not exempted from the other examinations prescribed by canon law, if they are exacted in the diocese to which he belongs.

The privilege of teaching is the very basis of the doctorate. There are, however, other honorary privileges attached to the degree, as that of wearing a four-horned biretta and a gold ring. Some important dignities and offices in the Church are likewise reserved for doctors.

2. The title of *Doctor* is given by a university which has received from the Holy See the power of conferring academic degrees. Degrees conferred by other than apostolic authority are not recognized by the Church, and the recipients of such degrees are not entitled to any canonical privileges.

The titles most usually granted to priests are those of Doctor of Theology, Doctor of Philosophy, Doctor of Sacred Scripture, Doctor of Canon (or Civil) Law, Doctor of both Laws (in utroque), and Doctor of Sacred Mush.

These titles may be written in full after the Doctor's name, or be indicated by initials. These initials are the following:

Doctor of Theology: D. D. (*Doctor Divinitatis*), or S. T. D. (*Sacrae Theologies Doctor*).

Doctor of Philosophy: Ph. D. (*Philosophiae Doctor*).

Doctor of Canon Law: D. C. L. (*Doctor of Canon Law*), or J. C. D. (*Juris Canonici Doctor*).

Doctor of Civil Law: J. C. D. (*Juris Civilis Doctor*), and LL. D. (*Doctor of Laws*).

Doctor of both Laws: J. U. D. (*Juris Utriusque Doctor*).

Doctor of Sacred Scripture: S. S. D. (*Sacrae Scriptures Doctor*).

Doctor of Sacred Music: Mus. D. (*Musicae Doctor*).

3. The principal mark of a Doctor's dignity is the four-horned biretta. This is not a choir cap; therefore, it should not be worn with the choir habit, or in church functions. A Doctor is allowed to wear his cap only when acting as Doctor, namely, when teaching, attending academic solemnities, etc. [1]

The doctoral biretta given by the Roman universities is of plain black silk. Some other universities have adopted different designs of doctoral birettas. Thus the biretta of Louvain is black, with a tuft of a color proper to each department of sacred sciences. The Doctors of Theology of the Catholic University of America, Washington, D.C., wear a doctoral biretta of black velvet, with red silk lining, trimmings and tuft.

All Bishops have the title "D. D." But this title does not carry with it the right of wearing a purple four-horned biretta. The purple biretta has been granted by Pope Leo XIII. as an exterior mark of the episcopal character, not as a sign of academic distinction. [2] The biretta conceded is a choir biretta, therefore, three-horned, and its shape can not be changed. Moreover, even with only three horns, this biretta is sufficient to indicate that the Bishop is a Doctor, since it is understood that all Bishops are Doctors. Again, a Doctor must wear no other doctoral biretta than that conferred on the Doctors of the university of which he is a graduate. Now, no university, to my knowledge, includes the purple biretta among the insignia of its Doctors.

Finally, the Archbishop of Santiago (Chile) having asked whether he might use a four-horned biretta, the Sacred Congregation of Rites answered in the negative. [3]

Although the clerical biretta and the doctoral cap are very similar in shape, they differ as to the origin and meaning, and therefore, should not be confounded. No one is ever allowed to wear his doctoral biretta, with his choir habit, or to add one more horn to his choir biretta under the pretext of manifesting his doctorate.

4. Another mark of the Doctorate is the gold ring. For doctors of the Roman College it is a plain ring, with the word ROMA carved on the bezel. [4] In other universities, the doctoral ring is adorned with a gem. There is no written law prohibiting a doctor from wearing a gemmed ring. If he is a doctor in several branches, he may even wear several rings, one for each doctorate. [5]

The doctoral ring is worn on the same finger as the prelatial ring, namely, on the fourth finger of the right hand.

Doctors may wear the ring everywhere, at all times, except when saying Mass or performing ecclesiastical functions. The Sacred Congregation of Rites, on several occasions, has given explicit and categorical answers to questions on this point. [6]

5. Besides these privileges, the doctorate is also desirable, because, according to the discipline of the Council of Trent, some ecclesiastical dignities and offices are reserved for Doctors. Such are the dignities of Chapters, [7] the functions of a Vicar Capitular, [8] those of an Archdeacon, [9] the office of Examiners of the clergy. [10] Above all, the doctorate is required in the candidates for the episcopacy. [11]

However, for all these dignities, the licenciate is accepted as a substitute for the doctorate. Candidates may even be dispensed from that requirement of the Council. Ordinarily, they obtain a dispensation if they are not doctors, or sometimes receive from Rome a doctor's diploma, together with their bulls of institution.

[1] S. R. C., Decem. 7, 1844, in Venusina. "*Nec uti posse, in ecclesiasticis junctionibus, tali bireto.*"
[2] Const. *Praeclaro divinae gratiae,* Feb. 3, 1888. S. R. C., Dec. 7, 1844.
[3] S. R. C., Sept. 5, 1895.
[4] A. Battandier, *Annuaire Pontifical* (1906), p. 449. - Barbier de Montault, *op. cit.*, Tom. I., pp. 159, 171, 172. Grimaldi, *op. cit.*, ch. XXIII.
[5] Cfr. the interesting discussion of this point in Battandier's *Annuaire Pontifical, loc. cit.*
[6] S. R. C, May 22, 1612 - Febr. 12, 1625 - Nov. 1628 - March 3, 1674 - May 23, 1846, etc.
[7] Benedict XIII., Const. *Pastoralis officii* (May 19, 1725).
[8] Council of Trent, Sess. XXIV., ch. XVI.
[9] Council of Trent, Sess. XXIV, ch. XII.
[10] Council of Trent, Sess. XXV, ch. XVIII.
[11] Council of Trent, Sess. XXII., ch. II., de *Reformatione.*

Documents

Decree of Pope Pius X. Concerning the Privileges of Roman Prelates

PIUS PP. X.
MOTU PROPRIO.

DE PROTONOTARIIS APOSTOLICIS, PRAELATIS URBANIS, ET ALIIS.
QUI NONNULLIS PRIVILEGIIS PRAELATORUM PROPRIIS FRUUNTUR.

Inter multiplices curas, quibus ob officium Nostrum apostolicum premimur, ilia etiam impomtur, ut venerabilium Fratrum Nostrorum, qui episcopali charactere praefulgent, pontificales praerogativas, uti par est, tueamur. Ipsi enim Apostolorum sunt Successores; de us loquitur Cyprianus (*ep.* 69, n. 8) dicens, *Episcopum in Ecclesia esse et Ecclesiam in Episcopo;* nec ulla adunatur Ecclesia sine Episcopo suo, imo vero Spintus ipse Sanctus *posuit Episcopos regere Ecclesiam Dei* (*Act. XX,* 38.) Quapropter, *Presbyteris superiores esse Episcopos,* iure defmivit Tridentinum Concilium (*Sess. XXIII,* c. 7). Et licet Nos, non tantum honoris, sed etiam mrisdictionis pnncipatum supra ceteros Episcopos, ex Christe dispositione, tamquam Petri Successores, geramus, nihilominus Fratres Nostri sunt Episcopi, et sacra Ordmatione pares. Nostrum ergo, est, illorum excelsae dignitati sedulo prospicere, eamque pro viribus coram christiano populo extollere.

Ex quo praesertim Pontincalmm usus per Decessores Nostros Romanos Pontifices aliquibus Praelatis, episcopali charactere non insignitis, concessus est, id saepe accidit, ut, vel malo hommum mgenio, vel prava aut lata nimis interpretatione, ecclesiastica disciplma haud leve detrimentum ceperit, et episcopalis dignitas non parum injuriae.

Quum vero de humsmodi abusibus ad hanc Apostolicam Sedem Episcoporum querelae delatae sunt, non abnuerunt Praedecessores Nostri iustis eorum postulationibus satisfacere, sive Apost. Littens, sive S. Rit. Congr. Decretis pluries ad rem editis. In id maxime intenderunt Benedictus XIV, per epist. S. R. Congr. d. d. 31 Martii MDCCXLIV, "*SSmus Dominus Noster*", iterumque idem Benedictus, d. 17 Februarn MDCCLII "In throno iustitics;" Pius VII, d. 13 Decembris MDCCCXVIII "Cum innumeri," et rursus idem Pius, d. 4 lulii MDCCCXXIII "*Decet Romanos Pontifices*", et Pius IX, d. 29 Augusti MDCCCLXXII "*Apostolicae Sedis officium.*" E Sacr. Rit. Congregatione memoranda in primis Decreta quae sequuntur: de Praelatis Episcopo infenonbus, datum die 27 mensis Septembris MDCLIX et ab Alexandro VII connrmatum; dein Decreta diei 22 Aprilis MDCLXXXIV de Canomcis Panormitanis; diei 29

Ianuarn MDCCLII de Canonicis Urbinatibus; diei 27 Aprilis MDCCCXVIII de Protonotariis Titularibus, a Pio PP. VII approbatum; ac diei 27 Augusti MDCCCXXII de Canonicis Barensibus.

Hisce tamen vel neglectis, vel ambitioso conatu, facili aufugio amplificatis, hac nostra aetate saepe videre est Praelatos, immoderato insignium et praerogativarum usu, praesertim circa Pontificalia, viliores reddere dignitatem et honorem eorum, qui sunt revera Pontifices.

Quamobrem, ne antiquiora posthabeantur sapienter a Praedecessoribus Nostris edita documenta, quin imo, ut iis novum robur et efficacia adiiciatur, atque insuper praesentis aevi indoli mos iuste geratur, sublatis omnibus consuetudinibus in contrarium, nec non amplioribus privilegiis, praerogativis, exemptionibus, indultis, concessionibus, a quibusvis personis, etiam speciali vel specialissima mentione dignis, nominatim, collective, quovis titulo et iure, acquisitis, assertis, aut praetensis, etiam Praedecessorum Nostrorum et Apostolicae Sedis Constitutionibus, Decretis, aut Rescriptis, confirmatis, ac de quibus, ad hoc, ut infirmentur, necesse sit peculiariter mentionem fieri, exquisito voto aliquot virorum in canonico iure et liturgica scientia peritorum, reque nature perpensa, motu proprio, certa scientia, ac de Apostolicae potestatis plenitudine, declaramus, constituimus, praecipimus, ut in posterum, Praelati Episcopis inferiores aliique, de quibus infra, qua tales, non alia insignia, privilegia, praerogativas audeant sibi vindicare, nisi quae hoc in Nostro documento, motu proprio dato, continentur, eademque ratione ac forma, qua hie subiiciuntur.

A. - de Protonotariis Apostolicis.

1. Quatuor horum habeantur ordines: I. Protonotarii Apostolici de Numero Participaritium, septem qui Col legium privative constituunt; II. Protonotarii Apostolici Supranumerarii; III. Protonotarii Apostolici ad instar Participantium; IV. Protonotarii Apostolici Titulares, seu honorarii (extra Urbem).

I. Protonotarii Apostolici de Numero Participantium

2. Privilegia, iura, praerogativas et exemptiones quibus, ex Summorum Pontificum indulgentia iamdudum gaudet Collegium Protonotanorum Apostohcorum de numero Participantium, in propriis Statutis nuperrime ab ipsomet Collegio iure reformatis inserta, liber.ter confirmamus, prout determmata invenmntur in Apostolicis Documentis inibi citatis, ac praesertim in Constitutione *"Quamvis peculiaris"* Pii Pp. IX, diei 9 mensis Februarii MDCCCLIII, paucis exceptis, quae, uti infra, moderanda statuimus:

3. Protonotarii Apostolici de numero Participantium habitu praelatitio rite utuntur, et alio, quem vocant *pianum* atque insignibus prout infra numeris 16, 17, 18 describuntur.

4. Habitu quotidiano incedentes, caligas, collare et pileum ut ibidem n. 17 gestare poterunt, ac insuper Annulum gemmatum, quo semper iure utuntur, etiam in privatis Missis aliisque sacris functionibus.

5. Quod vero circa usum Pontificalium insignium, Xystus V in sua Constitutione *"Laudabilis Sedis Apostolicae sollicitudo,"* diei 6 mensis Februarii MDCLXXXVI, Protonotariis Participantibus, concessit: "Mitra et quibuscumque aliis Pontificalibus insignibus, etiam in Cathedralibus Ecclesiis, de illorum tamen Praesulum, si praesentes sint, si vero absentes, absque illorum consensu, etiam ilis irrequisitis, extra curiam uti", in obsequium praestantissimae Episcoporum dignitatis, temperandum censuimus, ut pro Pontificalibus, extra Urbem tantum agendis, iuxta S. R. C. declarationem quoad Episcopos extraneos vel Titulares, diei 4 mensis Decembris MCMIII, ab Ordinario loci veniam semper exquirere teneantur, ac insuper consensum Praelati Ecclesiae exemptae, si in ea sit celebrandum.

6. In Pontificalibus peragendis, semper eis inhibetur usus throni, pastoralis baculi et cappae; item septimi candelabn super altan, et plunum Diaconorum assistentia; Faldistorio tantum utentur, apud quod sacras vestes assumere valeant. Pro concessis enim in citata Xysti V Constitutione, "quibuscumque aliis pontificalibus insignibus, non esse sane intelligenda declaramus ea, quas ipsis Episcopis extra Dicecesim sunt interdicta. Loco *Dominus vobiscum* numquam dicent *Pax vobis;* trinam benedict Jonem impertientur numquam, nec versus illi praemittent *Sit nomen Domini et Adiutorium,* sed in Missis tantum pontifi calibus, Mitra cooperti, cantabunt formulam *Benedical vos,* de more populo benedicentes; a qua benedictione abstinebunt, assistente Episcopo loci Ordmario, aut alio Praesule, qui ipso Episcopo sit maior, ad quem pertinet earn impertiri.

7. Ad Ecclesiam accedentes, Pontificalia celebraturi, ab eaque recedentes, habitu praelatito induti, supra Mantelletum Crucem gestare possunt pectoralem, a qua alias abstinebunt; et nisi privatim per aliam portam ingrediantur, ad fores Ecclesiae non excipientur ut Ordinarius loci, sed a Caeremoniano ac duobus clencis, non tamen Canonicis seu Dignitatibus; seipsos tantum aqua lustrali signabunt, tacto, aspersorio illis porrecto, et per Ecclesiam procedentes populo numquam benedicent.

8. Crux pectoralis, a Protonotariis Participantibus in pontificalibus functionibus adhibenda, aurea erit, cum unica gemma, pendens a funiculo serico *rubini* coloris commixto cum auro, et simili flocculo retro ornato.

9. Mitra in ipsorum Pontificalibus erit ex tela aurea (numquam tamen pretiosa) quae cum simplici alternari possit, iuxta Caerem. Episcop. (*I, XVII, nn.* 2 *et* 3); nec alia Mitra nisi simplici cliebus pcenitentialibus et in exsequiis eis uti hcebit. Pileolo nigri coloris sub Mitra dumtaxat uti poterunt.

10. Romae et extra, si ad Missam lectam cum aliqua solemrutate celebrandam accedant, habitu praelatitio induti, praeparationem et gratiarum actionem persolvere poterunt ante altare, in genuflexorio pulvinaribus tantum mstructo, vestes sacras ab altan assumere, aliquem clericum *in Sacris* assistentem habere, ac duos Jnferiores ministros. Fas erit praeterea Canonem et Palmatoriam, Urceum et Pelvim cum Manutergio in lance adhibere. In aliis Missis lectis, a simplici sacerdote ne differant, nisi in usu Palmatoriae. In Mis-

sis autem cum cantu, sed non pontificalibus uti poterunt etiam Canone et Urceo cum Pelvi et lance ad Manutergmm.

11. Testimonium autem exhibere cupientes propensas voluntatis Nostrae in pennsignem hunc coetum, qui inter cetera praelatorum Collegia primus dicitur et est in Romana Curia, Protonotariis Participantibus, qui a locorum Ordinarns sunt exempti, et ipsis Abbatibus praecedunt, facultatem facimus declarandi omnibus qui Missae ipsorum intererunt, ubivis celebrandae, sive in oratoriis privatis, sive in altan portatili, per eiusdem Missae auditionem diei festi praecepto rite planeque satisfieri.

12. Protonotarius Apostolicus de numero Participantum, qui ante decimum annum ab adepto Protonotariatu Collegium deseruerit, aut qui a decimo saltern discesserit, et per quinque alios, iuxta Xysti V Constitutionem, iisdem privilegiis gavisus fuerit, inter Protonotarios *ad instar* eo ipso erit adscnptus.

II. Protonotarii Apostolici Supranumerarii

13. Ad hunc Protonotariorum ordinem nemo tamquam privatus aggregabitur, sed iis tantum aditus fiet, qui Canonicatu potiuntur in tribus Capitulis Urbis Patriarchalium, id est Lateranensis Ecclesiae, Vaticanae ac Libenanae; itemque iis qui Dignitate aut Canonicatu potiuntur in Capitulis aliarum quarumdam extra Urbem ecclesiarum, quibus privilegia Protonotanorum *de numero* Apostolica Sedes concesserit, ubique fruenda. Qui enim aut in propria tantum ecclesia vel dioecesi titalo Protonotarii aucti sunt, aut nonullis tantum Protonotanorum privilegns fuerunt honestati neque Protonotariis aliisve Praelatis Urbanis accensebuntur, neque secus habebuntur ac illi de quibus hoc in Nostro documento nn. 80 et 81 ent sermo.

14. Canonici omnes, etiam Honorarii, turn Patriarch alium Urbis, turn aliarum ecclesiarum de quibus supra, tamquam singuli, msigmbus et lunbus Protonotanorum ne fruantur, nec gaudeant nomine et honore Praelatorum, nisi pnus a Summo Pontifice inter Praelatos Domesticos per Breve adscripti smt, et alia servaverint quae infra num. 34 dicuntur. Protonotarius autem *ad instar,* qui Canonicis emsmodi ascenseatur, eo ipso privilegia Protonotarii Supranumerani acquiret.

15. Protonotarii Apostolici Supranumerarii subjecti remanent propno Ordmano, ad forman Conciln Tndentim (*Sess.* 24, *c.* 11), ac eorum beneficia extra Romanam Curiam vacantia Apostoiicae Sedi minime reservantur.

16. Habitum praelatitium gestare valent coloris violacei, in sacns functionibus, id est caligas, collare, talarem vestem cum cauda, nunquam tamen explicanda, neque in ipsis Pontificahbus celebrandis: sencam zonam cum duobus flocculis panter sencis a laeva pendentibus, et Palholum, seu Mantelletum supra Rocchetum; insuper nigrum biretum flocculo ornatum coloris *rubini:* pileum item nigrum cum vitta senca, opere reticulato exornata, eiusdem *rubini* coloris cuius coloris et serici erunt etiam ocelli, globuli, exiguus torulus collum et anteriores extremitates vestis ac Mantelleti exornans, eorum subsutum, itemque reflexus (*paramani*) in manicis (etiam Roccheti).

17. Alio autem habitu uti poterunt, Praelatorum proprio, vulgo *piano,* in Congregationibus, conventibus, solemnibus audientiis, ecclesiasticis et civilibus, idest caligis et collan violacei coloris, veste talari nigra cum ocellis, globulis, torulo ac subsuto, ut supra, *rubini* coloris, serica zona violacea cum laciniis pariter sericis et violaceis, peramplo palho talari item senco violaceo, non undulato, absque subsuto aut ornamentis quibusvis alterius coloris, ac pileo nigro cum chordulis et sericis flocculis *rubini* coloris Communi habitu incedentes, caligas et collare violacei coloris ac pileum gestare poterunt, ut supra dicitur.

18. Propriis Jnsignibus seu stemmatibus imponere po terunt pileum cum lemmscis ac flocculus duodecim, sex hinc, sex inde pendentibus, eiusdem *rubini* coloris, sine Cruce vel Mitra.

19. Habitum et insignia in choro Digmtates et Canonici Protonotarii gerent, prout Capitulo ab Apostolica Sede concessa sunt; poterunt nihilominus veste tantum uti violacea praelatitia cum zona sub chorahbus insignibus, nisi tamen alia vestis tamquam insigne chorale sit adhibenda. Pro usu Roccheti et Mantelleti in choro attendatur, utrum haec sint speciah indulto permissa; alias enim Protonotarius, praelatitio habitu assistens, neque locum inter Canonicos tenebit, neque distributions lucrabitur, quae sodahbus accrescent.

20. Cappam laneam violaceam, pellibus ermelhni hiberno tempore, aestivo autem *rubini* coloris serico ornatam, Jnduent in Cappellis Pontificiis, in quibus locum habebunt post Protonotarios Participates. Ii vero Canonici Protonotarii qui Preelati non sunt, seu nomine tantum Protonotanorum, non vero omnibus iuribus gaudent, ut nn. 13 et 14 dic tum est, in Cappellis locum non habebunt, neque ultra limites pontificiae concessionis habitu praelatitio et *piano,* de quibus nn. 16 et 17, uti umquam poterunt.

21. Habitu praelatitio induti, clencis quibusvis, Presbyteris, Canonicis, Dignitatibus, etiam collegialiter unitis, atque Praelatis Ordinum Regularium, quibus Pontificalium privilegium non competat, antecedunt, mmime vero Vicariis Generalibus vel Capitulanbus, Abbatibus et Canonicis Cathedralium collegialiter sumptis. Ad Crucem et ad Episcopum non genuflectent, sed tantum sese inclmabunt: duplici ductu thurificabuntur: item si sacris vestibus induti functionibus in choro adsistant.

22. Gaudent mdulto Oratorn privati dorm rurique, ab Ordinario loci visitandi atque approbandi, in quo, etiam solemnioribus diebus (exceptis Paschatis, Pentecostes, Assumptionis B. M. V., SS. Apostolorum Petn et Pauli, nec non loci Patroni principalis festis) celebrare ipsi Missam poterunt, vel alms Sacerdos, in propnam, consangumeorum, affinium, famihanum et cohabitantium commoditatem, etiam ad prseceptum implendum. Privilegio autem altaris portatilis ommno carere se sciant.

23. Licet iisdem acta conficere de causis Beatificationis et Canonizationis Servorum Dei, quo tamen privilegio uti non poterunt, si eo loco alter site Collegio Protonotanorum Participantium.

24. Rite eliguntur in Conservatores Ordinum Regularium ahorumque piorum Institutorum, in Iudices Synodales, in Commissaries et Iudices Apostolicos etiam pro causis beneficialibus et ecclesiasticis. Item apud ipsos professionem Fidei recte emittunt, qui ex officio ad earn adiguntur. Ut autem mnbus et praerogativis, hie et num. 23 expressis, frui possint Canonici Protonotarii in S. Theologia aut in iure Canonico doctorali laurea insigniti sint oportet.

25. Extra Urbem, et impetrata venia Ordinarii loci, cui ent arbitrium earn tribuendi quoties et pro quibus Solemnitatibus voluent, atque obtento etiam consensu Praelati ecclesiae exemptae, in qua forte celebrandum sit, pontificali ritu Missas et Vesperas aliasque sacras funo tiones peragere poterunt. Quod functiones attinet collegialiter, seu Capitulo praesente, celebrandas, a proprns Constitutionibus, de Ordinarii consensu, provideatur, mxta Apostolica Documenta.

26. - Ad ecclesiam accedentes, Pontificalia celebraturi, ab eaque recedentes, habitu praelatitio induti, supra Mantelletum Crucem gestare possunt pectoralem (a qua alias abstinebunt): et nisi privatim per aliam portam ingrediantur, ad fores ecclesiae non excipientur ut Ordinarius loci, sed a Caeremoniano et duobus clericis, non tamen a Canonicis seu Dignitatbus: seipsos tantum aqua lustrali signabunt, tacto aspersorio sibi porrecto, et per ecclesiam procedentes populo numquam benedicent.

27. Pontificalia agent ad Faldistorium, sed vestes sacras in sacrario assument et deponent, quae in Missis erunt: *a*) Caligae et sandalia serica cum orae textu ex auro; *b*) Tunicella et Dalmatica; *c*) Crux pectoralis sine gemmis, e chordula serica *rubini* ex integro coloris pendens, auro non intertexta, simili flocculo retro ornata; *d*) Chirothecae sericae, sine ullo opere phrygio, sed tantum orae textu auro distinctae; *e*) Annulus cum unica gemma; *f*) Mitra ex senco albo, sine ullo opere phrygio, sed tantum cum orae textu ex auro, et cum laciniis simihter aureis, quae cum simplici ex lino alternari poterit, iuxta Caerem. Episcopor. (*I, XVII, nn.* 2 et 3); haec vero simplex, diebus poenitentialibus et in exsequiis una adhibebitur; *g*) Canon et Palmatoria, a qua abstinendum coram Ordmano seu maiori; *h*) Urceus et Pelvis cum Mantili in lance; *i*) Gremiale.

28. In Vesperis solemnibus (post quas benedictionem non impertientur) aliisque sacris functionibus ponticaliter celebrandis, Mitra, Cruce pectorali, Annulo utentur, ut supra. Pileolus nigri dumtaxat coloris, nonnisi sub Mitra ab eis poterit adhiberi.

29. In pontificalibus functionibus eisdem semper interdicitur usus throni, pastoralis baculi et cappae; in Missis autem pontificalibus, septimo candelabro super altari non utentur, nec plurium Diaconorum assistentia; Presbyterum assistentem pluviali indutum habere poterunt, non tamen coram Episcopo Ordinario aut alio Praesule, qui ipso Episcopo sit maior; mtra Missam manus lavabunt ad Ps. *Lavabo* tantum. Loco *Dominus Vobiscum,* nunquam dicent *Pax vobis;* trinam benedictionem impertientur nun quam, nec

versus illi praemittent *Sit nomen Domini* et *Adiutorium,* sed in Missis tantum pontificalibus, Mitra cooperti, cantabunt, formulam *Benedicat vos,* de more populo benedicentes: a qua benedictione abstmebunt assistente Episcopo loci Ordinario aut alio Praesule, qui ipso Episcopo sit maior, cuius ent earn impertin. Coram iisdem, in pontificalibus celebrantes, Mitra, simplici solummodo utantur, et dum illi sacra sumunt paramenta, aut solium petunt vel ab eo recedunt stent sine Mitra.

30. de speciali commissione Ordinani, Missam quoque pro defunctis pontificali ritu celebrare poterunt Protonotarii Supranumerarii, cum Absolutione in fine, Mitra linea utentes; numquam tamen eamdem Absolutionem impertiri illis fas erit, post Missam ab alio celebratam; quod ius uni reservatur Episcopo loco Ordinario.

31. Romae et extra, si ad Missam lectam cum aliqua solemnitate celebrandam accedant, habitu praelatitio induti, praeparationem et gratiarum actionem persolvere poterunt ante altare in genuflexorio pulvinaribus tantum mstructo, vestes sacras ab altari assumere (non tamen Crucem pectoralem et Annulum) aliquem clericum *in Sacris* assistentem habere, ac duos inferiores ministros; Canonem et Palma toriam, Urceum et Pelvim cum Manutergio in lance adhibere; sed ante v. *Communio* manus ne la vent. In aliis Missis lectis a simplici Sacerdote ne differant, nisi in usu Palmatoriae: in Missis autem cum cantu, sed non pontificalibus, uti poterunt etiam Canone, Urceo cum Pelvi, ac lance ad Manutergium nisi ex statutis vel consuetudme in propna ecclesia haec prohibeantur.

32. Canonico Protonotario Apostolico Supranumerario pontificalia peragere cum ornamentis ac ntu supenus enunciatis fas non erit, nisi infra terminos propriae dicecesis; extra autem, nonisi ornatu et ritu, prout Protonotariis *ad instar,* ut infra dicetur, concessum est.

33. Cum tamen Canonicos trium Patriarchalium Urbis ob earumdem praestantiam, aequum sit excellere privilegiis, eo vel magis quod in Urbe, ob Summi Pontificis praesentiam, Pontificalium privilegium exercere nequeunt, illis permittitur, ut in ecclesns totms terrarum orbis, impetrata Ordinariorum venia, ac Praesulum ecclesiarum exemptarum consensu, Pontificalia agant cum ritu atque ornamentis nn. 27, 28, 29 recensitis. Insuper, licet aliquis ex ipsis inter Praelatos nondum fuent adscriptus, Palmatona semper, etiam in privatis Missis uti poterit.

34. Recensita hactenus privilegia ilia sunt quibus dumtaxat Protonotani Apostolici Supranumerarn fruuntur. Verum, cum eadem collective ccetui Canonicorum conferantur, Canomci ipsi, tamquam smguli, us uti nequibunt, nisi Praelati Urbani fuerint nominati et antea suae ad Canonicatum vel Dignitatem promotionis et auspicatae iam possessionis, atque inter Praelatos aggregations, ut num. 14 dicitur, testimonium Collegio Protonotariorum Participantium exhibuerint; coram ipsius Collegii Decano, vel per se vel per legit Jmum procuratorem, Fidei professionem et fidelitatis iusiurandum de more praestiterint, ac de his postea, exhibito documento, propnum Ordmanum

certiorem fecerint. Quibus expletis, eorum nomen in sylloge Protonotariorum Apostohcorum recensebitur.

35. - Canonici ecclesiarum extra Urbem, qui ante Nostri huius documenti Motu Proprio editi publicaticnem, privilegia Protonotariorum, una cum Canonicatu, sunt assequuti, ab expeditione Brevis, de quo supra, num. 14, dispensantur; iusiurandum tamen fidelitatis coram Ordinario suo praestabunt infra duos menses.

36. Collegialiter tamquam Canonici pontificalibus functionibus, iuxta Caeremoniale Episcoporum, sacris vestibus induti adsistentes non alia Mitra utantur, quam simphci, nec unquam hoc et ceteris fruantur Protonotariorum insignibus et privilegiis extra propriam ecclesiam, nisi in diplomate concessionis aliter habeatur. Canomcus tamen qui forte ad ordinem saltern Subdiaconatus non sit promotus, neque in choro cum alus Mitra unquam utatur. In functionibus autem praedictis inservientem de Mitra non habebunt, prout in Pontificalibus uni Celebranti competit. Qui in Missa solemni Diaconi, Sudbiacom, aut Presbyten assistentis munus agunt, dum Dignitas, vel Canonicus, aut alter Privilegiarius pontifica.iter celebrant, Mitra non utentur; quam tamen adhibere poterunt Episcopo solemniter celebrante, ut dictum est de collegialiter adsistentibus, quo in casu ministrant, aut cum Episcopo operantur, maneant detecto capite.

37. Protonotarius Supranumerarius defunctus efferri aut tumulari cum Mitra non poterit, neque haec eius feretro Jmponi.

38. Ne autem Protonotariorum numerus plus aequo augeatur, prohibemus, ne in posterum in ecclesiis, de quibus supra, Canonici Honorarii, sive infra, sive extra Diaecesim degant, binas partes excedant eorum, cui Capitulum iure constituunt.

39. Qui secus facere, aliisve, praeter memorata, privilegiis et iuribus uti praesumpserint, si ab Ordinario semel et bis admoniti non paruerint, eo ipso, Protonotariatus titulo, honore, iuribus et privilegus, tamquam singuli, privates se noverint.

40. Sciant praeterea, se, licet forte plures una simul, non tamquam unius ecclesiae Canomci, sed tamquam Prctonotarii conveniant, non idcirco Collegium praelatitium constitueri; verum quando una cum Protonotariis de numero Participantium concurrunt, v. gr. in Pontificia Cappella, tune quasi unum corpus cum ipsis effect. censentur, sine ullo tamen amplissimi Collegii praeiudicio, ac servatis eiusdem Cappellae et Familiae Pontificiae consuetudmibus.

41. Si quis (exceptis Canonicis trium Patriarchalium Urbis) quavis ex causa Dignitatem aut Canonicatum dimittat, cui titulus, honor et praerogativae Protonotarii Apostolici Supranumerarii adnexa sint, ab eiusmodi titulo, honore et praerogativis statim decidet. Qui vero Pontificium Breve inter Praelatos aggregationis obtinuerit, horum tantum privilegiis deinceps perfruetur.

III. Protonotarii Apostolici Ad Instar

42. Inter Protonotarios Apostolicos *ad instar* Partici pantium illi viri ecclesiastici adnumerantur, quibus Apostolica Sedes hunc honorem conferre voluerit, ac praeterea Dignitates et Canonici alicuius Capituli praetantioris, qui bus collegialiter titulus et privilegia Protonotariorum, cum addito *ad instar*, ubique utenda, fuerint ab eadem Apostolica Sede collata. Canonici enim qui aut in propria tantum ecclesia vel dioecesi titulo Protonotarn aucti sunt, aut nonnulis tantum Protonotariorum privilegiis fuerunt honestati, neque Protonotariis aliisve Praelatis Urbanis accensebuntur, neque secus habebuntur ac illi de quibus hoc in Nostro documento nn. 80 et 81 erit sermo.

43. Qui Protonotarii Apostolici *ad instar* tamquam singuli iuribus honorantur, eo ipso sunt Praelati Domus Pontificiae; qui vero ideo sunt Protonotarii quia alicuius ecclesiae Canonici, Praelatis Domesticis non adnumerantur, nisi per Breve Pontificium ut num. 14 dictum est. Omnes Protonotarii *ad instar* subiecti remanent, ad iuris tramitem, Ordinario loci.

44. Beneficia illorum, qui Protonotarii *ad instar* titulo et honore gaudent tamquam Canonici alicuius Capituli, si vacent extra Romanam Curiam, Apostohcae Sedi minime reservantur. Beneficia vero eorum, qui tali titulo et honore fruuntur, tamquam privata persona, non poterunt nisi ab Apostolica Sede conferri.

45. Quod pertinet ad habitum praelatitium, *pianum* et communem, stemmata et choralia insignia, habitum et locum in Pontificia Cappella, omnia observabunt, uti supra dictum est de Protonotariis Supranumerariis, nn. 16, 17, 18, 19, 20.

46. Iisdem iuribus gaudebunt, praecedentiae, privati oratorii, conficiendi acta Beatificationis et Canonizationis, passivae electionis in Conservatores, cetensque; item recipiendae Fidei professionis, reverentiae ad Crucem, thurificationis, quibus omnibus fruuntur Protonotarii Supranumerarii, ut supra nn. 21, 22, 23, 24, ac iisdem sub conditionibus.

47. de venia Ordinarii et Praesulis consensu ecclesiae exemptae, extra Urbem, Missas, non tamen de requie, pontificali ritu et ornatu celebrare poterunt, prout supra notatur, ubi de Protonotariis Supranumerariis, nn. 25; 26, 27, 28, 29; verum his legibus: Nec Faldistorio nec Gremiali unquam utantur, sed una cum Mmistris in scamno, cooperto panno coloris diei, sedeant; caligis et sandaliis utantur sericis tantum, cum orae textu item serico flavi coloris ornato, et similiter sericis chirothecis sine alio ornamento; Mitra simplici ex serico damascene, nullo ornamento, ne in ons quidem distmcta, cum rubns laciniis ad vittas. Extra Cathedrales Ecclesias tantum, assistentem Presbyterum habere poterunt pluviali indutum, dummodo non assistat Episcopus Ordmarms aut alms Praesul ipso Episcopo maior. Crucem pectoralem auream sine gemmis gerent, appensam funiculo serico violacei ex integro coloris, auro non intertexto. Omnia, quae in Missa cantanda vel legenda

sunt, nunquam ad scamnum, sed ad altare cantabunt et legent. Manus infra Missam lavent tantum ad Ps. *Levabo.*

48. Poterunt insuper, pariter extra Urbem, de venia Ordinarii et cum Praesuli ecclesiae exemptae consensu, Mitra, Cruce pectorali et Annulo ornati, ad scamnum, more Presbyterofum, celebrare Vesperas illius festi, cuius Missam ipsi pontificaliter acturi sint, vel peregerint (absque benedictione in fine). Iisdem ornamentis eodemque ritu uti licebit, de speciah tamen commissione Ordinarii, in Vesperis festi, cuius Missa in pontificalibus ab alio quolibet Praelato celebretur, itemque in benedictione cum Sanctissimo Sacramento solemmter (non tamen trine] impertienda, in Processionibus, et in una ex quinque absolutionibus in solemnioribus exsequiis, de quibus in Pontificali Romano.

49. Romae Missam lectam aliqua cum solemnitate celebrantes, si preelatitio habitu sint induti, ea retineant, quae de Protonotariis Supranumerariis n. 31 constituta sunt; extra Urbem, de speciali tamen commissione Ordinarii, eodem modo se gerent; aliis in Missis et functionibus, tamquam Praelati Domestici, ut n. 78, Palmatoriam tantum, si velint, adhibeant.

50. Qui Canonicorum ccetui adscnptus, cui hactenus recensita Protonotariorum *ad instar* privilegia concessa sint, tamquam privata persona iisdem uti velit, prius Breve Pontificium, ut dicitur nn. 14 et 43, de sua inter Praelatos Domesticos aggregatione, servatis servandis, obtineat, simulque suae ad Canonicatum vel Dignitatem prcmotionis, initaeque possessionis ac inter Praelatos aggregationis testimonium Collegio Protonotariorum Participantium exhibeat. Tum coram ipsius Collegii Decano, vel per se vel per legitimum procuratorem, Fidei professionem ac fidelitatis iusiurandum, de more, praestet; de his denique exhibito documento proprium Ordinarium certiorem faciat. Qui vero tamquam privata persona huiusmodi titulum rite fuerit consecutus, non ante privilegiis eidem titulo adnexis uti potent, quam legitimum suae nominationis testimonium memorato Collegio exhibuerit, Fidei professionem et fide litatis iusiurandum, uti supra, ediderit, de hisque omnibus authenticum documentum suo Ordinario attulerit. Haec ubi praestiterint, eorum nomen in sylloge Protonotariorum recensebitur.

51. Qui ante has Litteras, motu proprio editas, iuribus gaudebant Protonotarii *ad instar,* tamquam alicuius ecclesiae Canonici, a postulaticne Brevis, de quo in superiori numero, dispensantur, quemadmodum et a iureiurando, ut ibidem dicitur, praestando, quod tamen proprio Ordinario infra duos menses dabunt.

52. Habitum et insignia in choro Dignitates et Canonici Protonotarii gerent, prout Capitulo ab Apostolica Sede concessa sunt; poterunt nihilominus veste tantum uti violacea praelatitia cum zona sub choralibus insignibus, nisi tamen alia vestis, tamquam insigne chorale sit adhibenda. Pro usu Roccheti et Mantelleti in choro attendatur, utrum haec sint speciali indulto permissa; alias enim Protonotarius, habitu praelatitio assistens, neque locum inter Canonicos tenebit, neque distributiones acquiret, quae sodalibus accrescent.

53. Collegialiter tamquam Canonici pontificalibus functionibus iuxta Caeremoniale Episcoporum, sacris vestibus induti assistentes, non alia Mitra utentur quam simplici, nec unquam hoc aliisve supra memoratis insignibus et, privilegiis extra propriam ecclesiam, nisi in concessionis diplomate aliter habeatur. Canonicus tamen, qui forte ad ordinem saltern Subdiaconatus non sit promotus, ne in choro quidem cum aliis Mitra unquam utatur. In functionibus autem praedictis inservientem de Mitra non habebunt, prout in Pontificalibus uni Celebranti competit. Qui in Missa solemni Diaconi, Subdiaconi aut Presbyteri assistentis munus agunt, dum Dignitas, vel Canonicus, aut alter Privilegiarius pontificaliter celebrant, Mitra non utentur; quam tamen adhibere poterunt, Episcopo solemniter celebrante, ut dictum est de collegialiter adsistentibus, quo in casu, cum ministrant, aut cum Episcopo operantur, maneant detecto capite.

54. Protonotarius *ad instar* defunctus eflerri aut tumulari cum Mitra non poterit, nec eius feretro ipsa imponi.

55. Ne autem Protonotariorum numerus plus aequo augeatur, prohibemus, ne in posterum in ecclesiis, de quibus supra, Canonici Honorarii, sive infra, sive extra Dioecesim degant, binas partes excedant eorum, qui Capitulum iure constituunt.

56. Qui secus facere, aliisve, praeter memorata, privi legiis et iuribus uti praesumpserint, si ab Ordinario semel et bis admoniti non paruerint, eo ipso, Protonotariatus titulo, honore, iuribus et privelegiis, tamquam smguli, pri vates se noverint.

57. Sciant praeterea; se, licet forte plures una simul, non tamquam unius ecclesiae Canonici, sed tamquam Protonotarii, conveniant, non idcirco Collegium Praelatitum constituere; verum, quando una cum Protonotariis de numero Participantium concurrent, v. gr. in Pontificiis Cappellis, tune quasi unum corpus cum ipsis censentur, sine ullo tamen amplissimi Collegii praeiudicio, ac servatis eiusdem Cappellae et Familiae Pontificiae consuetudinibus.

58. Si quis, quavis ex causa, Dignitatem aut Canonicatum dimittat, cui titulus, honor et praerogativae Protonotariorum *ad instar* adnexa sint, statim ab iisdem titulo, honore et praerogativis decidet. Qui vero Pontificium Breve inter Praelatos aggregationis obtinuerit, horum tantum privilegiis deinceps perfruetur.

IV. Protonotarii Apostolici Titulares Seu Honorarii

59. Cum Apostolica Sedes, non sibi uni ius reservaverit Protonotarios Titulares seu honorarios nominandi, sed Nuntns Apostolicis, Collegio Protonotariorum Participantium et forte aliis iamdiu illud delegaverit, antequam de eorum privilegiis ac praerogativis aliquid decernamus, leges seu conditiones renovare placet, quibus rite honesteque ad eiusmodi dignitatem quisque Canditatus valeat evehi, iuxta Pii PP. VII Praedecessoris Nostri Constitutionem *"Cum innumeri"*, Idibus Decembr. MDCCCXVIII datam.

60. Quoties igitur de honorario Protonotariatu assequendo postulatio praebeatur, proferantur, ab Ordinario recognita, testimonia, quibus constet indubie: (1) de honesta familiae conditione; (2) de aetate saltern annorum quinque et viginti; (3) de statu clericali ac caelibi; (4) de Laurea doctoris in utroque, aut canonico tantum iure, vel in S. Theologia, vel in S. Scriptura; (5) de morum honestate et gravitate, ac de bona apud omnes aestimatione; (6) de non communibus in Ecclesiae bonum provehendum laudibus comparatis; (7) de idoneitate ad Protonotariatum cum decore sustinendum, habita etiam annui census ratione, iuxta regionis cuiusque aestimationem.

61. Quod si huiusmodi Protonotariatus honor alicui Canonicorum coetui collective ab Apostolica Sede conferatur (quod ius, collective Protonotarios nominandi, nemini censeri posse delegatum declaramus), eo ipso, quo quis Dignitatem aut Canonicatum est legitime consequutus, Protonotarius nuncupabitur.

62. Pariter, qui Vicarii Generalis aut etiam Capitularis munere fungitur, hoc munere dumtaxat perdurante, erit Protonotarius Titularis; hinc, si Dignitate aut Canonicatu in Cathedrali non gaudeat, quando choro interesse velit, habitu Protonotarn praelatitio, qui infra describitur, iure utetur.

63. Protonotarii Apostolici Titulares sunt Praelati extra Urbem, qui tamen subiecti omnmo manent locorum Ordinariis, Praelatorum Domus Pontificiae honoribus non gaudent, neque inter Summi Pontificis Familiares adnumerantur.

64. Extra Urbem, dummodo Summus Pontifex eo loci non adsit, in sacris functionibus rite utuntur habitu prae latitio, nigri ex integro coloris, idest veste talari, etiam, si libeat, cum cauda (nunquam tamen explicanda), zona serica cum duobus flocculis a laeva pendentibus, Roccheto, Martelleto et bireto, absque ulla horum omnmo parte, subsuto aut ornamento alterius coloris.

65. Extra Urbem, praesente Summo Pontifice, descripto habitu indui possunt, si hie tamquam chorale insigne concessus sit, vel si quis uti Vicarius adfuerit.

66. Habitu praelattio induti, omnibus Clericis, Presbyteris, etiam Canonicis, singulatim sumptis, praeferantur, non vero Canonicis, etiam Collegia tarum, collegialiter convenientibus, neque Vicariis Generalibus et Capitularibus, aut Superioribus Generalibus Ordinum Regularium, et Abbatibus, ac Praelatis, Romanae Curiae; non genuflectunt ad Crucem vel ad Episcopum, sed tantum se inclinant, ac duplici ductu thurificantur.

67. Super habitu quotidiano, occasione solemnis conventus, audientiae et similium, etiam Romae et coram Summo Pontifice, zonam tantum sericam nigram, cum laciniis item nigris, gestare poterunt, cum pilec chordula ac floccis nigris ornato.

68. Propriis insignibus, seu stemmatibus, pileum imponere valeant, sed nigrum tantummodo, cum lemniscis et sex hinc sex inde flocculis pendentibus, item ex integro nigris.

69. Si quis Protonotarius Titularis, Canonicatus aut Dignitatis ratione, choro intersit, circa habitum se gerat iuxta normas Protonotariis *ad instar* constitutas, num. 52, vestis colore excepto.

70. Sacris operantes, a simplicibus Sacerdotibus minime differant; attamen extra Urbem in Missis et Vesperis solemnibus, pariterque in Missis lectis alhsque functionibus solemnius aliquando celebrandis Palmatoria tantum ipsis utenda conceditur, excluso Canone aliave pontificali supellectili.

71. Quod pertinet ad acta in causis Beatificationis et Canonizationis, et ad passivam electionem in Conservatores ac cetera, iisdem iuribus gaudent, quibus fruuntur Protonotarii Supranumerarii, uti nn. 23 et 24 supra dictum est.

72. Beneficia eorum qui, tamquam privatae personae, Protonotariatum Titularem assequuti sunt, non vero qui ratione Vicariatus, Canonicatus sive Dignitatis eodem gaudent, ab Apostolica tantum Sede conferantur.

73. Noverint autem, se, licet forte plures una simul, non tamquam unius ecclesiae Canonici, sed tamquam Proto notarii, conveniant, non ideo Collegium constituere.

74. Tandem qui Protonotariatu Apostolico honorario donati sunt, tamquam privatae personae, titulo, honoribus, et privilegus Protonotariatus uti nequent, nisi antea diploma suae nominationis Collegio Protonotariorum Participantium exhibuerint, Fideique professionem, ac fidelitatis iusiurandum coram Ordinario, aut alio viro in ecclesiastica dignitate constitute emiserint. Qui vero ob Canonicatum. Dignitatem, aut Vicariatum, eo potiti fuerint, nisi idem praestiterint, memoratis honoribus et privilegiis, quae superius recensentur, tantummodo intra proprise dioecesis limites uti poterunt.

75. Qui secus facere, aliisque, praeter descripta, privilegiis uti praesumpserint, si ab Ordinario semel et bis admoniti non paruerint, eo ipso honore et iuribus Protonotarii privatos se sciant: quod si Protonotariatum, tamquam privata persona adepti sint, etiam titulo.

76. Vicarii Generales vel Capitulares, itemque Dignitates et Canonici nomine atque honoribus Protonotariatus titularis gaudentes, si, quavis ex causa, a munere, Digni tate aut Canonicatu cessent, eo ipso, titulo, honoribus et iuribus ipsius Protonotariatus excident.

B. de Ceteris Praelatis Roman ae Curiae.

77. Nihil detractum volumus honoribus, privilegiis, praeeminentiis, praerogativis, quibus alia Praelatorum Romanae Curiae Collegia, Apostolicae Sedis placito, exornantur.

78. Insuper concedimus, ut omnes et singuli Praelati Urbani seu Domestici, etsi nulli Collegio adscripti, ii nempe, qui tales renunciati, Breve Apostolicum obtinuerint, Palmatoria uti possint (non vero Canone aut alia pontificali supellectili) in Missa cum cantu, vel etiam lecta, cum aliqua solemnitate celebranda; item in Vesperis aliisque solemnibus functionibus.

79. Hi autem habitum, sive praelatitium sive quern vocant *pianum,* gestare poterunt, iuxta Romanae Curiae consuetudinem, prout supra describitur nn. 16, 17; numquam tamen vesti talaris caudam explicare, neque sacras vestes ex altari assumere valeant, nec alio uti colore, quam violaceo, in bireti flocculo et pilei vitta, opere reticulate distincta, sive chordulis et flocculis, etiam in pileo stemmatibus imponendo ut n. 18 dictum est, nisi, pro eorum aliquo, constet de maiori parti culari privilegio.

C. - de Dignitatibus, Canonicis et Aliis, Qui Nonnullis Privileges Praelatorum Propriis Fruuntur.

80. Ex Romanorum Pontificum indulgentia, insignia quaedam praelatitia aut pontificalia aliis Collegiis, praesertim Canonicorum, eorumve Dignitatibus, quocumque nomine nuncupentur, vel a priscis temporibus tribui consueverunt; cum autem eiusmodi privilegia dimmutionem quamdam episcopali dignitati videantur affere, idcirco ea sunt de iure strictissime interpretanda. Huic principio inhaerentes, expresse volumus, ut in pontincalium usu nemini ad aliquod ex supra memoratis Collegiis pertinenti in posterum ampliora suffragentur privilegia, quam quae, superius descripta, competunt Protonotariis sive Supranumerariis, sive *ad instar,* et quidem non ultra propriae ecclesiae, aut ad summum Dioeceseos, si hoc fuerit concessum, limites; neque ultra dies iam designates, aut determinatas functiones; et quae arctiora sunt, ne augeantur.

81. Quoniam vero de re agitur haud parvi momenti, quippe quae ecclesiasticam respicit disciplinam, ne quis audeat arbitraria interpretatione, maiora quam in concedentis voluntate fuerint, sibi privilegia vindicare; quin potius paratum sese ostendat, quatenus ilia excessennt minoribus coarctari; singulis locorum Ordinariis, quorum sub iurisdictione vel quorum in territorio, si de exemptis agatur, aliquis ex praedictis coetibus inveniatur, demandamus, ut, tamquam Apostolicae Sedis Delegati, Apostolicarum Concessionum documenta ipsis faventia, circa memorata privilegia, infra bimestre tempus, ab hisce Nostris Ordinationibus promulgates, sub poena immediatae amissionis eorum quae occultaverint, ad se transmitti curent, quae intra consequentem mensem ad Nostram SS. Rituum Congregationem mittant. Haec autem, pro suo munere, omnia et singula hisce Nostris dispositionibus aptans, declarabit et decernet, quaenam in posterum illis competant.

Haec omnia rata et firma consistere auctontate Nostra volumus et iubemus; contrariis non obstantibus quibuscumque.

Datum Romae apud S. Petrum, die 21 Februarii MCMV, Pontificatus Nostri anno secundo.

PIUS PP. IX.

135

Brief of Pope Pius IX, Granting to All Bishops the Privilege of Wearing a Purple Skull-Cap

PIUS PP. IX.

Ad perpetuam rei memoriam.

Ecclesiarum omnium curam et sollicitudinem ex supremo Apostolatus officio divina Providentia commisso gerentes, maximo quidem solatio perfundimur, cum ad sacrum episcopalem ordinem oculos Nostros mentemque convertimus.

Sacri enim per orbem Antistites, pastoralis muneris Nostri consortes in tanta temporum difficultate, atque in tot malorum procellis, quibus Ecclesia iactatur, omnem adhibent alacritatem ac studium in custodiendo vigilias noctis super gregem suum, in Ecclesiae iuribus adserendis, atque in christiana sibi concredita plebe divinae Legis praeceptionibus erudienda, ut hoc scilicet instructa munimine, facilius a malo declinet atque ambulet in viis Domini.

Ipsi propterea nullum discrimen detrectantes, opponunt murum pro domo Israel, interque ipsos, non pauci, persecutionem passi propter iustitiam, illustria suae fidei et fortitudine exempla ediderunt.

Quo autem obsequio, quo devotionis studio iidem Venerabiles Fratres prosequantur beatissimi Petri Cathedram, in qua intregra est christianae religionis ac perfecta solielitas, et ad quam, propter potiorem principalitatem necesse est omnem convenire ecclesiam, innumerae amoris ac pietatis significationes, etiam typis consignatae et nunquam intermissae, pro ipsius incolumitate et exaltatione in suis dioecesibus preces, excitatique fideles ad rerum angustias quibus premimur, data stipe, recreandas, denique singularis eorum in Urbe Nostra frequentia luculentissime testantur.

Quare, in communi omnium ordinum laetitia ob saecularem memoriam martyrii sanctorum Apostolorum Petri et Pauli solemniter celebrandam, et ob nonullos Ecclesiae heroes sanctorum coelitum fastis adscribendos, gratum Nobis est eosdem Venerabiles Fratres, in pastorali Nostro exercendo munere socios atque adiutores, debito exornare laudis praeconio, eisdemque, per aliquam honoris adiectionem, propensi animi Nostri, ad dilectionis exhibere testimonium.

Itaque, auctoritate Nostra Apostolica, harum litterarum vi, omnibus et singulis Catholicae Ecclesiae Patriarchis, Archiepiscopis et Episcopis, tam praesentibus quam futuris, concedimus atque indulgemus ut ipsi in posterum, a primis tamen vesperis proxime futuri festi Sanctorum Apostolorum Petri et Pauli, pileolo violacei coloris uti libere ac licite possint et valeant.

Non obstantibus constitutionibus et sanctionibus apostolicis, ceterisque quamvis speciali et individua mentione ac derogatione dignis in contrarium facientibus quibuscumque.

Datum Romae, apud Sanctum Petrum, sub annulo Piscatoris, die XVII Iunii MDCCCLXVII, Pontificatus Nostri anno vicesimo secundo.

Brief of Leo XIII, Granting to All Bishops the Privilege of Wearing a Purple Biretta

Leo PP. XIII.

Ad perpetuam rei memoriam.

Praeclaro divinae gratiae munere effectum est, ut sacerdotalis Nostrae consecrationis diem quinquagesimo anno redeuntem, frequenti Episcoporum Venerabilium Fratrum Nostrorum corona septi, innumero fidelium ccetu stipati, quin et universe christiano orbe gestiente, celebrare potuerimus. Cui tantae celebritati fastigium impositum est maioribus coelitum honoribus, quos, divino Spiritu adspirante, suprema auctontate Nostra nonnullis eximiae sanctitatis viris solemni ritu attribuimus. Quae quidem omnia non uno Nobis nomine grata et periucunda fuerunt. Primo enim in spem adcucimur fore ut fidelium precibus ac novensilium sanctorum intercession propitiatus Deus, tot tantisque, quibus humana premitur societas, malis opportuna afferat remedia, optatamque mundo pacem ac tranquilitatem largiatur. Deinde vero ex eo laetamur quod innumerabiles observantiae et obsequii significationes, quibus Nos toto orbe fideles unanimi consensione prosecuti sunt turn ostendunt et antiquam pietatem et Apostolicae Sedis amorem christianis pectoribus alte manere defixum, turn in summa Venerabilium Fratrum sacrorum Antistitum laudem cedunt, quorum opera ac virtute in populis sibi commendatis et concreditis in tanta temporum perversitate Jta viget ac floret catholicae religionis cultus et huic Sedi ac Romano Pontifici sunt animi addicti atque coniuncti.

Nos, ne fausti huius eventus memoria intercidat, atque ut publicum aliquod benevolentise Nostrae testimonium Venerabihbus Fratnbus exhibeamus, externo honoris insigni universes terrarum orbis Antistites exornandos censuimus.

Quare, hisce litteris, Apostolica auctoritate Nostra, perpetuum in modum concedimus ut universi Patriarchae, Archiepiscopi et Episcopi birreto violacei coloris, hoc futurisque temporibus, uti libere et licite possint et valeant. Hoc ita illis proprium volumus, ut alius qui episcopali dignitate non sit insignitus, eiusmodi ornamento nullatenus potiri queat.

Non obstantibus constitutionibus et sanctionibus apostolicis ceterisque omnibus, licet speciali et individua mentione ac derogatione dignis, in contrarium facientibus quibuscumque.

Datum Romae, apud Sanctum Petrum, sub annulo Piscatoris, die III Februarii MDCCCLXXXVIII Pontificatus Nostri anno decimo.

M. CARD. LEDOCHOWSKI.

Bibliography

This does not profess to be a complete bibliography of the subject, but a list of works which may be usefully consulted on the various points treated in this book.

Baart (Rev. P.), *The Roman Court*. (Cincinnati, 1895.)

Barrier de Montault (Mgr. X.), *Le Costume et les usages ecclésiastiques selon la tradition Romaine*. (Paris, s. d.)

Barbier de Montault (Mgr. X.), *Oeuvres completes*. (Poitiers, 1889-1902.)

Barbier de Montault (Mgr. X.), *Les gants pontificaux*. (Tours, 1877.)

Barbier de Montault (Mgr. X.), *Traité pratique de la construction, de rameublement et de la decoration des églises*. (Paris, s.d.) [1899.]

Barbosa, *Iuris ecclesiastici universi libri tres*. (Lyon, 1650.)

Bargilliat, *Praelectiones iuris canonici*. (Paris, 1918.)

Battandier (Mgr. A.), *Annuaire pontifical catholique*. (Paris, yearly since 1898.)

Baudot, O. S. B., *Le Pallium*. (Paris, 1909.)

Bock, *Geschichte der liturg.* Gewander. (Bonn, 1856-62.)

Bona, *Rerum liturgicarum libri duo*. (Turin, 1745.)

Bonnani, S. J. (Filippo), *La Gerarchia ecclesiastica*. (Rome, 1720.)

Bonanni, S. J. (Filippo), *Catalogo degli Ordini religiosi*. (Rome, 1741.)

Bouix, de *Curia Romana*. (Paris, 1874.)

Bouix, de *Episcopo*. (Paris, 1873.)

Bouix, de *Papa*. (Paris, 1869.)

Branchereau, *Politesse et convenances ecclésiastiques*. (Paris, 1892.)

Cahier and Martin (S. J.), *Mélanges d'archéologie*. (Paris, (1856.)

Catalani, *Caeremoniale episcoporum*. (Rome, 1744.)

Catalani, *Pontificate romanum*. (Rome, 1850.)

Cheneau (S. S.), *Explanation of the Catholic Liturgy for the Laity*. (Baltimore, 1907.)

Cohello, *Notitia Cardinalatus*. (Rome, 1653.) Cox (J. Charles), English Church Furniture. (London, 1907.)

Daniel, *Codex liturgicus*. (Leipzig, 1847-53.)

Deloche (M.), *Le port des anneaux*. (Paris, s. d.)

Demay (G.), *Le costume au moyen âge d'après les sceaux*. (Paris, 1880.)

Druitt, *A Manual of Costume as Illustrated by Monumental Brasses*. (London, 1906.)

Durandus (Episcopus Mimatensis), *Rationale divinorum officiorum*. (Lyon, 1612.)

Enlart (Camille), *Le Costume*. (Paris, 1916.)

Fabre (with Goyau and Pératé), *Le Vatican*. (Paris, 1895).

Favrin, *Praxis solemnium functionum episcoporum, cum appendicibus pro abbatibus mitratis et protcnotariis apostolicis, iuxta ritum romanum* (Ratisbon, 1906.)

Ferraris, *Bibliotheca canonica.* (Rome, 1862, 1885, 1896.)

Fisquet. *Les cérémories de Rome* (Paris, 1871.)

Fleury (J. Rohault de), *La messe.* (Paris, 1889.)

Fortescue (Adrian), *The Ceremonies of the Roman Rite Described.* (London, 1918.)

Gardellini, *Decreta cuthentica S. C. R.* (Rome.)

Geramb (Baron), *Visit to Rome.* (Philadelphia, 1840.)

Goyau (with Fabre and Pératé), *Le Vatican.* (Paris, 1895.)

Grimaldi, *Les congrégations romaines.* (Sienna, 1890.) (On the Index.)

Harvey (A.). (See Cox.)

Herdt (J. B. de), *Praxis pontificalis.* (Louvain, 1892.)

Hulme, *The History, Principles and Practice of Heraldry.* (New York, 1898.)

Kenrick (Archbishop), *Form of the Consecration of a Bishop.* (Baltimore, 1866.)

Kirchmann (Johannes), de *Annulis.* (Leyden, 1672.)

Kraus (Dr. F. X.), *Geschichte der christlichen Kunst.* (Freiburg-im-B., 1897.)

Kraus (Dr. F. X.), *Real-Encyklopädie des christlichen Alterthümer.* (Freiburg-im-B., 1882-86.)

Kraus (Dr. F. X.), *Kirchenlexicon.* (Freiburg-im-B., 1886.)

Lerosey, *Manuel liturgique.* [Paris, 1890.)

Levavasseur, *Cérémonial selon ie rite romain.* (Paris, 1923.)

Levavasseur, *Fonctions pontificales.* (Paris, 1904.)

Macalister, *Ecclesicstical Vestments.* (London, 1896.)

Macklin (H.-W.), *The Brasses of England.* (London, 1907.)

Marriott, *Vestiarium christianum.* (London, 1868.)

Martène, O. S. B. (Dom E.), de *antiquis ecclesice ritibus.* (Antwerp. 1784.)

Martigny, *Dictionnaire des antiquites chrétiennes.* (Paris, 1877.)

Marti Nucci (Mgr Fio), *Manuale sacrarum caeremoniarum* (Rome, 1911.)

Muhlbauer, *Decreta authentica Congregationis sacrorum rituum.* (Munich, 1863.)

Nainfa (J. A.), *A Synthetical Manual of Liturgy* (Vigourel). (Baltimore, 1907.)

Narfon (Julien de), *Léon XIII intime.* (Paris, s. d.)

Narfon (Julien de), *Pie X.* (Paris, 1905.)

Pératé (with Goyau and Fabre), *Le Vatican.* (Paris, 1905.)

Phillips, *Kirchenrecht.* (1845-72.)

Flatus (S. J.), de *Cardinalis dignitate et officio.* (Rome, 1658.)

Pope (Thomas, Canon). *Holy Week in the Vatican.* (Dublin, 1871.)

Pugin, *Glossary of Ecclesiastical Ornament.* (London, 1868.)

Reussens, *Élements d'archéologie chrétienne.* (Paris, 1885.)

Rohault de Fleury. *La Messe.* (Paris, 1889.)

Rock (Dr.), *Hierurgia or the Holy Sacrifice of the Mass*. (Revised and edited by W. H. J. Weak). (London, 1900.)

Rock (Dr.), *The Church of our Fathers*. (London.)

Shahan, etc., *Catholic Encyclopedia*. (New York.)

Simon, de Boncourt, *Grammaire du Blason*. (Paris, 1885.)

Smith (S.), *Notes on the Second Plenary Council of Baltimore*. (New York, 1874.)

Smith and Cheetam, *A Dictionary of Christian Antiquity*. (Hartford, 1880.)

Stehle, O. S. B. (Aurelius), *Manual of Episcopal Ceremonies*. (Beatly, 1916.)

Soglia, *Institutiones iuris publici ecclesiastici*. (Rome, 1843.)

Taunton, *The Law of the Church*. (London, 1906.)

Trombetta (Luigi), de *iuribus et privilegiis praelatorum Romanae Curiae*. (Sorrento, 1906.)

Un Évêque Suffragant, *Cérémonial des évêques expliqué*. (Paris, 1856).

Vigourel, S. S. (Adrian), *Manuel synthétique de liturgie*. (Paris, 1906.)

Vives y Tuto (Card. Joseph), de *dignitate et officiis Episcoporum et Praelatorum*. (Rome, 1905.)

Wilpert (Mgr.), *Un capitolo di storia del vestiario*. (Rome, 1899.)

Wilpert (Mgr.), *Die Gewändung der Christen in der ersten Jahrhunderten*. (Cologne, 1898.)

Woodward, *Manual of Ecclesiastical Heraldry*. (London, 1894.)

Wuscher-Becchi, *Ursprung der papstlichen Tiara (regnum) und der bishoflichen Mitra*. (Rome, 1899.)

Wyllie (Col. Robert E.), *Orders. Decorations and Insignia, Military and Civil*. (New York, 1921.)

www.ingramcontent.com/pod-product-compliance
Lightning Source LLC
LaVergne TN
LVHW011356080426
835511LV00005B/313